the SECRET *of* Instant Healing

Frank J. Kinslow

Lucid Sea

Sarasota, Florida

This book is not intended to diagnose, prescribe or treat. The information contained herein is in no way to be considered as a substitute for care from a duly licensed healthcare professional.

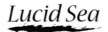

Lucid Sea

THE SECRET OF INSTANT HEALING
Previously Published by TRIAD Publishing Group
under ISBN: 13: 978-0-9815045-1-3

Cover and interior design by Edge Literary & Marketing Services

Library of Congress Number: 2008921314
Printed in the U.S.A.
Printed September 2008

To my Mom.
For my children,
Cyndi, Becky and Brad,
My sister
Sharon
And
Diana

Special Thanks

To "Badlands" Jimmy,
the fastest and most accurate editing gun in the west

And

Vern, friend and publisher extraordinaire

Also by Frank J. Kinsow
Beyond Happiness: How You Can Fulfill Your Deepest Desire

The Secret of Instant Healing

Table of Contents

Preface

Wʜᴀᴛ if I told you that just by being aware of a problem you can fix it? "Sure," you say, "I become aware of a problem and then I take steps to correct it. What's so special about that?"

That is pretty much the way life unfolds, isn't it? But that's not what I'm talking about. What if you just become aware of a problem and, with no more effort on your part, awareness did the fixing? Would that be special? Sure it would. And that is exactly what I am talking about. You can become aware of an arthritic knee, indigestion, or a headache, anger or fear, a failing relationship or the loss of a job, in just the right way, and the organizing genius of awareness will fix what is broken. That is not just special, that is a wonderment. It is a skill that could alter your world, and our planet, in unimaginable ways. It is a way of embracing life that would soften and enliven the world we live in, transforming it into the world of our dreams. Simply put, becoming aware of the healing and organizing force of awareness is the answer to the problems that have plagued us since we first stood erect and stepped headlong into the human condition.

If it seems to you that I have over inflated the role of awareness in attuning our lives to our inherent wisdom, I have not. And it will only take you a few minutes to discover the accuracy of my assertion. This is a small book wielding stupendous potential. But you don't have to take my word for it, not at all. What I am offering you is a scientifically reproducible process that anyone can do. All you need be is aware. Are you aware? Are you conscious of reading these words? Do you know if you are sitting or standing? Do you know what you are thinking right now? Then that settles it. You can learn the simple steps that refine your awareness and heal your body and mind. You can learn to heal the bodies and minds of others. And, with a little help from your friends, you are poised to transmute the ills of humankind on this earth.

Are you ready? Do you feel a sense of anticipation, a feeling of immanent discovery? What opens to you within the pages of this simple book will be your private journey. We will know its impact by the deeds you perform after its reading. The rest is easy. You have only to turn the page to forever change your life.

Thanksgiving Day, 2007
Sarasota, Florida

Chapter One

Beginning

"Anything will give up its secrets if you love it enough. I have found that when I silently commune with people they give up their secrets also, if you love them enough."
                                                                    George Washington Carver

There is a subtle secret that is waiting for you, closer than your next breath, more vital than your next heartbeat. Once you grasp this secret your life will open to wonders light years beyond what you thought possible. It is the secret to health and joy and peace, and it is working right now as you read these lines. But this secret is hidden from you. It is hidden, not within the symbols of an obscure parchment deep within the bowels of an ancient temple, but right before your open eyes.

This simple book will reveal that secret to you and show you how to draw from its depths to enrich your life and the lives of your family, friends and even your pets. In the pages that follow you will learn how to heal body, mind and soul as effortlessly as watching a poetic sunset. The scientific procedure that will unfold before you is easily learned and readily applied by all. It is as simple as the secret itself, and as powerful.

I recommend that you do not jump ahead, but read this book

page by page. It is in this way that the secret will find its home in your consciousness. Please take time do each exercise as it is presented. You will be learning a new skill and some practice is necessary for it to become second nature. The exercises are not difficult. In fact, they are delightful, nurturing and enlivening. So no matter how eager you are to start working wonders, take your time on the basics. As a wise teacher once shared, "Well begun is half done."

On your trek, you will first gain an understanding of what

This secret is hidden from you. It is hidden, not within the symbols of an obscure parchment deep within the bowels of an ancient temple, but right before your open eyes.

awareness is and where it can be found. Then you will meet your secret face to face and embrace it as an old friend. Finally, you will learn how to entice it out into your life to heal your body, harmonize your emotions and sharpen your mind, creating a more productive and joyful life. Of course, you will be able to share your secret with others, healing and enlivening their lives as well.

Chapter Two

The Secret Revealed

"The ultimate value of life depends upon awareness and the
power of contemplation rather than upon mere survival."
Aristotle

I would like to ask you a simple question. Understanding the answer could change your life forever. Think it through thoroughly. Then continue reading. Here is the question: *What is most important to you in this life?*

What did you come up with? Health? Family? Mind? Job? Ice cream? My answer to this question is awareness. Without awareness you have nothing. You cannot love your spouse and children, work at your job or sip coffee on a sidewalk café without awareness. For all intents and purposes, without awareness you do not exist.

Awareness is not your mind. If your mind were a light bulb, then awareness would be the electricity that lights it up. A dull reflection of awareness in the mind causes confusion, misunderstanding and ultimately suffering. A mind bright with awareness is calm and present. It displays a peaceful gentleness that puts others at ease. If you look at awareness as your "inner light" you will be close to understanding its vital importance.

The quality of your awareness determines the quality of your life.

The quality of your awareness determines the quality of your life. It is important that your awareness be vibrant and awake. Let's say you are sitting in a completely dark room next to a window. It is pre-dawn but light is just starting to enter the room when you look down to see an unidentifiable form at your feet. Fascinated, you continue to watch as, little by little, the room lightens and you begin to see the object more clearly. All at once and to your horror, you realize the object is a coiled snake ready to strike. You are immobilized, afraid to move for fear the snake will strike a moving target. Your mind is firing off frantic thoughts like "Is the snake poisonous? If I move a muscle will it strike? If I'm bitten how will I get help?" You sit stone still as the light continues to slowly lighten the room. You note that for some reason the snake has not yet struck. You begin to relax a little and think more clearly. Your mind quickly reviews escape scenarios while your body remains rigid and unmoving. The sun crests the horizon and the first rays of dawn break through the window filling the room with a delicate golden light. Then, like the brightness of lightning on the blackness of night, you see that the snake is actually a coiled rope.

You felt fear. Your mind froze and then shattered, thoughts scattered broken glass. All the while your rigid body was pumping stress hormones into your blood, preparing you for battle.

In those few moments you may have aged months. Why? Simply because you perceived a threat where there was none.

We can equate the darkness with impaired awareness. Overwork or lack of exercise, drugs, alcohol, poor diet, or anger, greed or grief, all dampen consciousness and impair our ability to perceive our world in a nonthreatening way.

Our lives are filled with perceived threats. We have financial snakes, job snakes, family snakes. Even while driving to a pleasant event like a movie or the beach, traffic can ruin the mood, boiling blood pressure and exploding tempers. We are the "fight or flight" generation perceiving snakes around every corner.

How do we change those perceptions? How do we enjoy the full light of day, exposing those snakes for the ineffectual ropes that they are? Why, we become more aware. Awareness is like sunlight. It lightens the emotions and enlightens the mind. Dull minds and muddy emotions are poor reflectors of awareness. Perception is fueled by our awareness. Pure awareness can never be fooled by a rope.

We are the "fight or flight" generation perceiving snakes around every corner.

Most of the time our minds are on autopilot. Incessant mental chatter is a good example of a runaway mind. The hyperactive mind, so common today that it is considered normal, wastes vast amounts of energy and continually gets us into trouble. Other symptoms include worrying about the future or dwelling on the past, boredom, frustration, anger, anxiety and fear. These are all ropes that look like snakes. Dull awareness makes our world a fearful place.

Awareness is everywhere all the time, but we just don't pay attention to it. I know that sounds a little weird but it's true. Normally we are preoccupied with things and people and thoughts that makeup our everyday lives. We are aware of those things but are we aware of awareness? Not often. Most of us wouldn't know pure awareness if it walked right up and shook your hand. That is all about to change.

Awareness is everywhere all the time, but we just don't pay attention to it.

Wait a minute. That's it? That's the secret? Awareness? You are probably feeling a little disappointed right now. I would too if I thought that I could own the secret to the universe simply by identifying what happens when it is in short supply. You may not have a very clear idea of what I'm talking about, either. That is because pure awareness can not be captured in the mind's eye. You can't take a picture of pure awareness. Awareness is not a thing or idea or emotion. So talking about it can be frustrating if you want to own it with your mind. It's not physical so you can't grab awareness and use it like a hammer. However, once you have experienced, or actually non-experienced, pure awareness directly, all this will make perfect and beautiful sense.

If you are a little confused at this point don't worry. You do not have to understand anything about awareness to make it work wonders in your life. That said, it will be valuable to have some knowledge about awareness to explain to others why they can feel so good, so fast. As you will soon discover, you will be creating miracles and having fun and pure awareness will be as natural to you as breathing. OK, ready for a little book learnin'? Good.

You do not have to understand anything about awareness
to make it work wonders in your life.

Chapter Three

Awareness and the Universe

"Let us not look back in anger or forward in fear, but around in awareness."
James Thurber

"The moment one gives close attention to anything, even a blade of grass, it becomes a mysterious, awesome, indescribably magnificent world in itself."
Henry Miller

First take a look at *Figure 1: The Material Model* on page 9. Start by noting the horizontal line near the bottom of figure 1. That line represents the division between the phenomenal world of created things and the no-thing from which they were created. Above is the infinity of creation and below the unbounded abode of pure awareness.

Pure awareness is one, without form. That means it has no boundaries that our minds can identify. Our minds work with things that can be recognized by their differing forms. Minds are the containers for thoughts and emotions. Through our senses our minds are kept in contact with the material world. We can distinguish a bagel from a bullfrog by their differences. That may seem rather simplistic but the mind's job is to identify different forms, label and categorize them, then use them or file them for future use.

Pure awareness is one, without form.
That means it has no boundaries that our minds can identify.

This whole process is accomplished by thought, which is a form. Thoughts and emotions are mental forms. Ideas, beliefs, hopes and philosophies are an assemblage of thoughts around a central theme much as a chair is an assemblage of molecules around the idea of supporting you in a sitting position. Thoughts

Figure 1:
Material Model

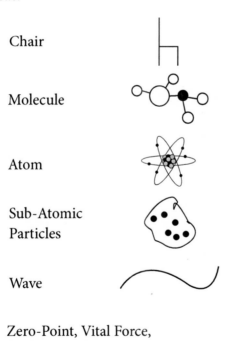

Chair

Molecule

Atom

Sub-Atomic
Particles

Wave

Zero-Point, Vital Force,
Eufeeling

Pure Awareness

Impicate Order, Nothing, Unexpressed Love, Non-Experience

are not as tangible as material objects but they are objects none-theless. The point here is that all things in the universe are indi-vidual and unique. Each object is separated and identified by its unique form.

Below the horizontal line we find that pure awareness has no form. Think of it as the blank page on which the words are to be written. Awareness is formless, unbounded, undifferentiated, and pure. It is one without a second. Because pure awareness is formless it cannot be recognized by our minds. No matter how hard you try, you will not be able to understand awareness. Neither will you be able to control or manipulate it. It doesn't exist as a thing, so as far as your mind is concerned, it does not exist. But it does.

So here is the task we have ahead of us. We must find some-thing with no form or substance. Then we must come to know this "no-thing" more intimately than we know our own minds. Finally, we must use this unusable non-force to heal ourselves and others. Are you beginning to realize why this knowledge is secret? This secret exists because we live in our minds, unaware of awareness. Despite a lifetime of experience to the contrary, we believe our minds when they tell us that lasting joy, peace and love come from things. We fall for that old trick time and time again. And we believe our minds when they tell us that no-thing has no value. But it does.

Despite a lifetime of experience to the contrary, we believe our minds when they tell us that lasting joy, peace and love come from things.

Pure awareness has no boundaries so there is nothing that can change about awareness. That kind of nothing lasts forever. All other things, which means all of creation, change and eventually cease existing. Change is the only constant in the created realm. The instant a thing is created it begins its journey to extinction. Pure awareness never changes, never dies. It is the field of undying love and unbounded peace.

Now here's the kicker. Everything that has form comes out of formless pure awareness. Don't ask me how, it just does. Out of the womb of pure awareness is spun the web of creation. Quantum physics has discovered the realm of pure awareness, theoretically at least. David Bohm, one of the foremost theoretical physicists of his generation, identified an "unbounded whole" in which is contained an implicate order. This is not to be confused with the zero-point field or quantum state which is the lowest energy state of a particle or object. The state that Bohm is referring to has no energy. Plainly stated, this field contains the "stuff" of creation silently waiting to become form or energy. So what Bohm is telling us is that everything comes from nothing. He is saying that, and I'm making a bit of an inductive leap here, creation springs out of the nothing of pure awareness. You will actually experience this later when you learn how to stop your thinking, then watch your thoughts materialize again out of nothing. Now let's turn our eye back toward phenomenal creation found above the horizontal line.

Everything in creation expresses two qualities: order and energy. Let's use the chair you are sitting in to demonstrate this point. What you call your chair is actually energy in the form of a chair. We know it exhibits energy because your chair keeps your derriere in the air. (I love poetry, don't you?) Order, in the energy/order equation, is expressed by the form of your chair. So it doesn't matter if we are referring to stars or atoms, amoebas or zebras, everything is energy and form.

Out of the womb of pure awareness is spun the web of creation.

The most basic created form is the wave. Just before the wave, and just after pure awareness on the creation hierarchy, you will find the zero-point field or quantum state. I add this tidbit for those who are familiar with quantum theory and want to appreciate more fully my position. If you are oriented more toward the healing sciences this most basic level of creation is often referred to as the vital force, that which breathes life into organic existence. A wave is infinite, stretching out endlessly. Where waves overlap they create sub-atomic particles. When the particles become more compact they become atoms. Atoms huddle together to form molecules and molecules arrange themselves in physical forms like chairs and flowers and cars.

Everything in creation expresses two qualities: order and energy.

In our energy/order hierarchy, the more tangible the order of a thing is the less energy it expresses. Your chair is pretty solid compared to a sub-atomic particle. Sub-atomic particles are slippery little guys. If you know the exact location of a sub-atomic particle you don't know how fast, or in what direction it is moving. Likewise, if you clock its exact speed, you won't be able to find it. My kids were like adolescent sub-atomic particles right around chore time. If they were in motion, a necessary quality for completing chores, you couldn't find them. If you could define their exact position, i.e. on the couch in front of the TV, you couldn't get them moving. Looking back, it is amazing how many physics concepts my kids had mastered like inertia, entropy and particularly Heisenberg's Uncertainty Principle. I owe them a lot.

Okay, let's get back to the idea of energy and matter. Each subtler level of creation contains more energy. At the present gross material level, the energy of the chair you are sitting in supports your weight. At the subtler molecular level of the chair we will find more available energy. If we rearranged its molecules, say by setting it on fire, we could release a good deal more energy in the form of heat and light. If we want to release even more energy from the chair we can go to the atomic level. If we knew how to split the atoms of the chair we could release huge amounts of energy in many forms. I don't know of any

Each subtler level of creation contains more energy.

work around harnessing the power of sub-atomic particles but I do know of technologies that utilize subtle wave energy. This is the common abode of the energy healer and we will explore this very interesting work on our way to learning how to heal without energy.

Let me ask you this: Have you ever run out of thoughts? I

didn't think so. One thing we can say about thoughts is, from our first breath to our last they are always there. If thoughts are energy and we never run out of them, then it stands to reason that the source of thought is an inexhaustible source of energy. It also stands that we might benefit greatly if we could tap directly into our source of thought. It turns out that uncovering the source of your thought has a definite and overwhelmingly positive healing influence on physical ailments, personal relations, financial success, emotional fitness, and yes, even your love life. Every aspect of our lives is wonderfully transformed when we simply become aware of where it all begins. And that would be our ever-present companion pure awareness.

> *If thoughts are energy and we never run out of them,*
> *then it stands to reason that the source of thought*
> *is an inexhaustible source of energy.*

We just saw that the more refined levels of the material world yield more energy. But where did all that energy come from? By now we know it comes from pure awareness. Creation, by definition, is the movement of energy in some organized or orderly way. Here we need to understand a vital point: pure awareness is the source of energy without being energy. That means it does not move. It has the potential to create but it just hasn't done it yet. Neither does it have form. You could say that pure awareness is perfection waiting to express itself.

> *Pure awareness is the source of energy without being energy.*

Now you may be thinking, "Where is he going with all this?" I'm glad you asked. If you want to play solely in the relative field of life, by all means enjoy yourself. But if you want the greatest power and the most perfect order, you must contact the source of all knowledge, pure awareness. There are thousands of healing modalities that tap into the various levels of life. Body work and chiropractic are effective on the gross physical level. Herbs and medications work on the molecular level. Acupuncture and energy healing work with subtle energy waves. None of these healing forms are designed to draw directly from the source of creation. This book will teach you the science of healing from awareness. I call this process Quantum Entrainment. Remember, pure awareness is the source of energy and order and when you perform QE you are drawing from the purest, most powerful existent available. When you use Quantum Entrainment, you will not be doing the healing, awareness will. What's more, you will be healed along with the people you are helping. Talk about your win-win relationship.

Chapter Four

The Mind and Thoughts

"The ancestor of every action is a thought."
Ralph Waldo Emerson

"The question is: can you become aware of the reflex character of thought--that it is a reflex... And we could say that as long as the reflexes are free to change then there must be some kind of intelligence or perception, something a bit beyond the reflex, which would be able to see whether it's coherent or not."
David Bohm

Your mind is a created thing. It is not corporeal like your chair. It is mental rather than physical. But like matter your mind is energy and order. Your mind is the container for your thoughts. A thought is a very interesting phenomenon. When I was with Maharishi Mahesh Yogi in the early 70's, I spent five months meditating in the sleepy Spanish town of La Antilla. I meditated 10 – 12 hours every day. After the first few weeks my thoughts became very quiet and I began to see how my mind worked. During that time I cognized the birth of thought. Each newly created thought was a single point of bristling energy at the doorstep of pure awareness. I watched as it expanded to reveal its contents. Within each thought form was a vibration that represented emotion, logical thought, and each of the five senses. Every thought is a galaxy within the universe of mind. (*Figure 2: MENTAL MODEL*)

Figure 2:
Memtal Model

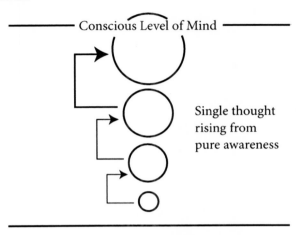

Conscious Level of Mind

Single thought
rising from
pure awareness

Pure Awareness

Once born, the thought would cut its umbilical cord with mother awareness and begin to rise and expand like a bubble rising from the bottom of a pond. The ego is born at this very instant when thought separates from fullness. As it expanded the thought energy became dispersed over a greater area. The thought became weaker the further it traveled away from its source. At this point it was susceptible to distortion and could become adulterated. Finally, the thought would burst like a bubble on the surface of my mind. The bursting of the thought bubble, Maharishi later told me, was when the mind became conscious of the thought at the end of its journey. It is at that point that we act on our conscious thoughts. I was simultaneously experiencing its birth and its death through an expanded awareness resulting from my meditation.

Your mind is the container for your thoughts.
Every thought is a galaxy within the universe of mind.

Each thought would have a dominant emotion and sensory vibration. As it expanded, the vibrations would interact and change. The thought would take its tendency toward action from the dominant inner vibrations. I also saw a kind of matrix through which thoughts would pass on their way to consciousness. If the inner workings had become distorted, this matrix could rearrange the inherent vibrations and change the tendency. Maharishi told me that this was the intellect filtering thoughts, helping to harmonize them so they would become more supportive to our health and well-being.

There is a lot to be taken away from this experience but for our purposes I would like to concentrate on a single point. The further a thought gets away from pure awareness, the weaker it becomes and the more likely it is to become harmful. What we call negative thoughts do not start out that way. They become misshapen by the imbalanced internal pressures of misconception and fear. Once a thought is born it experiences a kind of separation anxiety. The Bhagavad-Gita puts it this way: "Fear is born of duality." No longer attached to the unbounded oneness of awareness, a thought perceives that it is alone and tries to compensate for its loss. This is when distortion can infiltrate the otherwise perfectly functioning thought. An abhorrent thought is the cause of abhorrent action. We only have to look around

The further a thought gets away from pure awareness,
the weaker it becomes and the more likely it is to become harmful.

us to realize that a purely harmonious, loving and productive thought rarely finds expression in our day-to-day world.

If you think I am overly animating the life of a thought, or giving it too much intelligence, don't forget that it is the collection of these very thoughts that have brought you to where you are today. Most people take their basic identity from their thinking. You say, "I am successful in my job. I believe in free education. I am angry." But what was necessary for you to have success, beliefs and feelings? Every step of the way your thoughts have shaped and guided your progress, or lack thereof.

The further a thought has to go to work its way up to our consciousness, the more chance it has to become disharmonious. If we could expand our consciousness in such a way as to contact thought closer to its origin then we would diminish the likelihood of disharmony. This is not a new message. Sages have been telling us to get on this bandwagon for eons. The problem is not what to do, but how. Because we have not fully understood the role of awareness in thinking we have gotten ourselves in a pretty pickle. But it is more than understanding. Understand takes place in the mind. Pure awareness is beyond the mind. So understanding it is out of the question.

Most people take their basic identity from their thinking.

That leaves us with the experience of pure awareness. And that is a bit of a sticky wicket as well. To have an experience we need the mind. And herein lies one of the most salient and almost universally misunderstood tenets for knowing pure awareness. Pure awareness cannot be experienced. We know it by our lack of experience. I only want to mention this here. No amount of explaining will give us the non-experience of pure awareness. Presently, however, I will show you how to stop your thinking and discover for yourself where thoughts come from.

Pure awareness cannot be experienced.
We know it by our lack of experience.

Chapter Five

The Space Between Our Thoughts

*"We must learn to reawaken and keep ourselves awake,
not by mechanical aid, but by an infinite expectation of the dawn."*
Henry David Thoreau

*"If we could see the miracle of a single flower clearly,
our whole life would change."*
Buddha

The closer to pure awareness we contact a thought the more energy and order it has. Contacting a thought at its conception is realizing perfection, free of disharmonious influence. Before learning Quantum Entrainment you will be guided through several exercises that will open your common awareness to pure awareness. You only need tread the path once and you will ever after be aware of pure awareness. It will be like wearing a jacket on a chilly day. Once you put it on it will stay there keeping you toasty warm. Even when you forget you are wearing your jacket it is still protecting you. Any time you wish, you can become aware that you are wearing your jacket. Likewise, once you have found pure awareness you only have to become aware of it to know it is still with you. Are you ready to get started? Okay then, let's go.

Experience One: Stopping Thoughts

Sit comfortably and close your eyes. Now, pay attention to your thoughts. Just follow them wherever they may lead. Simply watch them come and go. After you have watched your thoughts for 5 to 10 seconds, ask yourself this question, and then be very alert to see what happens immediately after you ask. Here's the question: "Where will my next thought come from?"

What happened? Was there a short break in your thinking while you waited for the next thought? Did you notice a space, a kind of gap between the question and the next thought? OK, now reread the instructions, and perform the exercise again. I'll wait…

There, did you notice a slight hesitation in your thinking, a pause between thoughts? If you were alert immediately after you asked the question, you will have noticed that your mind was just waiting for something to happen. Author of *The Power of Now* Eckhart Tolle says it is like a cat watching a mouse hole. You were awake, waiting, but there were no thoughts in that gap. You may have heard that it takes many years of arduous practice to clear the mind of thoughts, but you have just done it in a matter of seconds.

Please do this exercise several more times. You can use substitute questions like "What color will my next thought be?" or "What will my next thought smell like?" or "What will my next thought look like?" The question is not important, but paying attention is. Attention will expose the gap, the space between thoughts. *This gap is pure awareness.* It may be fleeting, but it will be there. As you regularly become aware of this mental pause, it will begin to work its magic on you.

Now let's get back to work. Do this exercise for two to three minutes more, reintroducing the question every 15 seconds or so. Pay attention to the gap when it is there. Look for it when it is not. Within just a few minutes, you will notice that your thoughts are calmer and your body is more relaxed.

Why is that? You didn't set out to relax or become peaceful. It just happened naturally, without your trying. Why does becoming aware of awareness make such a big difference in the way we feel and behave? By being aware, you were able to contact your thoughts at subtler and more refined levels. Each level offers more order and energy. The gap you noticed between thoughts was the experience of no-experience I mentioned earlier. That non-experience was pure awareness. (*FIG 3: THE GAP*)

Figure 3:
The Gap

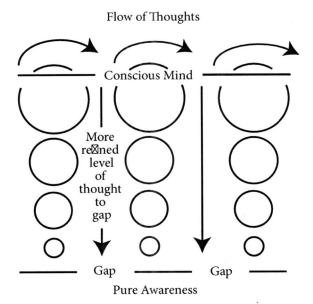

Flow of Thoughts

Conscious Mind

More refined level of thought to gap

Gap — Gap

Pure Awareness

Do a one-minute meditation, asking the mind a new question every 15 seconds, frequently throughout the day. You will soon become aware of the space that you found between your thoughts even while you are doing other activities like conversing or driving. If you were to do nothing more than regularly observe this brief interval between thoughts, over time you would notice more energy, less stress and even a fluid easiness in your relationships with others. You might even notice a lighter mood bordering on impishness. Feeling good is fun. This perception is the foundation for deeper, more fulfilling experiences to come. But even by itself this single exercise is worth the price of admission. Now let's expand on our knowledge of the source of thought to draw more deeply from its benefits.

The gap between thoughts was the experience of no-experience.
That non-experience was pure awareness.

Chapter Six
Who Am I

"The unexamined life is not worth living."
"The only true wisdom is in knowing you know nothing."
- Socrates -

A few years back Socrates urged us to "Know thy Self." Have you ever asked yourself why he felt that so very important? What possible benefits would befall us if we were to become acquainted with our Self? And what the heck is our Self anyway? Let's take a look.

Repeat *Experience One: Finding Pure Awareness*, and rediscover the gap between thought. Do it for several minutes, again asking one of the preparatory questions. Ask a question every 15 seconds or so, remembering to *be very alert to see what happens right after you ask the question.*

Experientially, this gap between thoughts is not much to write home about. It is just a space filled with stillness, obvious only after one thought ends and before the next thought begins. Since there is no thinking going on in the interval between thoughts, you won't be aware of it until you start thinking again, and maybe not even then. The mind follows the motion. It is enthralled with movement and form. The gap is free of both. It contains nothing. Nothing means, well, nothing to the mind.

But that is a big mistake. And here is why. All the thoughts in the mind come from that nothing which we have identified as pure awareness. Test it for yourself. Repeat the exercise and watch the gap. Automatically, and without any effort on your part, the next thought spontaneously arrives. There it is bright as day, a brand new thought. That's pretty miraculous when you stop to think about it. (Pun intended.) Each new thought is a marvel of creation and it comes from nothing. So nothing must not be empty. There must be something in that nothing, otherwise it could not produce a thought. Interesting, isn't it?

Since there is no thinking going on in the interval between thoughts,
you won't be aware of it until you start thinking again...

Repeat *Experience One* a couple more times. Above all, remember to be alert and wait to see what happens. By now, you are getting to be an old hand at observing the interval between your thoughts. Now, let me ask you the $64,000 question: Who is watching the gap? There are no thoughts, no emotions, no movement of any kind -- but you are still there, aren't you? You didn't go into a coma. You didn't go to Tacoma. You were right there waiting for thought to start up again, weren't you? Who was waiting? Who is this you? Who is watching when the mind disappears?

When you identify with your thoughts, all balled up in your memories and future plans, you are referring to the "me." "Me" is the collection of "things," like your age, your sex, your likes and loves, your hopes and memories that you call your life. But none of that exists at the moment your thoughts stop. To observe you must be aware, right? So at that moment when the mind is turned off you are aware of nothing. At that moment there is nothing but pure awareness. And now you have solved the mystery of who you are. You are awareness!

Who is watching when the mind disappears?

Does that sound impossible? The fact cannot be denied. Your direct perception has revealed your inner Self to be awareness. That's right, before "me" was born and built into the image you recognize as yourself, there was the solitary Self, pure awareness. This is what all the hubbub was about 2,500 years ago when Socrates was asking those probing questions. He made people examine not only the content of their thought, but the thoughts themselves. Of course you and I now know that leads very quickly to pure awareness, the indivisible inner Self.

Let's think a little longer on this business about us being pure awareness. Think back on your life. Take a moment and revisit your childhood and then some part of your adolescence. Now remember a time during your twenties, thirties, etc., until you reach your present age. Think about what you are doing right now. Over your lifetime your interests and feelings have changed, your body has grown and aged, family has matured and friends have come and gone. But there was a part of you that was with you as far back as you can remember and is with you still today. It has remained unchanged through all the phases of your life.

"Me" is the collection of "things," like your age, your sex, your likes and loves, your hopes and memories that you call your life.

At each stage of your life -- no, each second of your life -- while your body/mind was busy becoming what it is today, your awareness stood silent vigil, a timeless witness. When you said, "I want my mommy," "I hate gym class," "I will love you forever," or "I don't like loud music" you were identifying things, events and feelings that were happening to "me" but not to Self. The things and feelings of your life like wanting mommy, hating gym class, etc., all changed and now reside in that part of you called memory. The things of your life changed, and are changing still. But your awareness has remained an unmoving witness to the movie that you call your life.

Alfred Lord Tennyson spoke to this mystery of enduring changelessness in his poem *The Brook* when he penned, "Men may come and men may go, but I go on forever." We could just as easily but far less eloquently say my security, feelings, thoughts, body and environment may come and go but my awareness goes on forever. It certainly is not as stirring to the soul, but it does get the point across.

Why is knowing "Thy Self" so absolutely vital? When you come to appreciate your inner Self as unchanging, unbounded, eternal awareness, your dependence on the withering body and failing mind begins to loosen its hold. You become aware that you are beyond the field of change and death. You become aware that, beyond all the things and thoughts that "me" is, you eternally exist as awareness.

You are awareness!
Your awareness has remained an unmoving witness
to the movie that you call your life.

If just a few minutes of observing the gap between your thoughts brought peace and relaxation, imagine what joyful adventures await you when pure awareness infuses your thinking, eating, working and loving. Discovering yourself to be pure awareness at the bottom of your mind is the first step to living a full and bounteous life. Teasing awareness into daily activity is the next step. Finally, when you learn to heal your wounds and the wounds of others, it truly is a self-made blessing.

Chapter Seven
The Gate Technique

"If I had influence with the good fairy who is supposed to preside over the christening of all children, I should ask that her gift to each child in the world be a sense of wonder so indestructible that it would last throughout life."
- Rachel Carson -

I have witnessed all kinds of reactions when people discover that they are pure awareness and not the stuff and clutter their minds are filled with. Usually there is a moment of delighted surprise accompanied by a sense of freedom and lightness. That sense of euphoria can last for some time, but sooner or later the ego wants to take back control of its mind. When it does, thoughts and things are again elevated to their exalted and exaggerated position of importance. The frail echo of awareness fades into itself and is quickly forgotten. This does not have to happen. Hitting all the bases in this book will pretty much assure you of stabilizing pure awareness.

The next step to accomplish that end is to deepen and broaden the non-experience of pure awareness. We'll do that by increasing the amount of time we are aware of pure awareness. To do that, I have developed a wonderfully simple and effective process that anyone can do the very first time. I call it the Gate Technique because it opens the gate to pure awareness as easily

as if it had been oiled by the Keeper of the Gate himself. All we
need do is walk through.

*The next step is to deepen and broaden
the non-experience of pure awareness.*

The Gate Technique creates a subtle, yet profound shift in
the way we see our world. This "shift" may be barely noticeable
at first, and yet it will deeply influence your body/mind, and
from there, all other areas of your life. After just a few weeks of
doing the Gate Technique, it is not uncommon to have friends
comment on your relaxed features or the soft luminescence
reflecting in your eyes. It's time we got started, so roll up your
sleeves and get ready to open the gate to your Self.

*It is not uncommon to have friends comment on your relaxed
features or the soft luminescence reflecting in your eyes.*

Experience Two: The Gate Technique

(NOTE: You can download an audio MP3 version of the
Gate Technique at: *www.QuantumEntrainment.org*. I will lead
you through the Gate Technique step by step. For your ID use
your email address. For the password, enter *qe31*, all lowercase
with no spaces. You will also download the Pure Awareness
technique audio at that time. (See page 66) You will find this of
special value just before you learn Quantum Entrainment.)

*Sit in a comfortable chair where you will not be disturbed for
10 to 20 minutes. Close your eyes and let your mind wander for 10
to 20 seconds. Now go through a list of positive words in your mind.
You may see the words or hear them, it doesn't matter. Examples*

of these words might be: silence, stillness, calmness, peace, joy, bliss or ecstasy. You may also see or hear other words like: light, love, compassion, space, infinity, pure energy, existence or grace. After you have run through your list of positive words, go back over them. Gently pick a word that draws your attention. Now all you have to do is easily observe the word. Simply pay close attention and wait to see what it will do.

As you innocently watch, without interfering, your word will eventually change in some way. It may get bigger or brighter or louder. It might start pulsating or it may get fainter and even fade away and disappear. There is no telling what it will do but that doesn't matter. You job is to purely observe, without controlling or interfering in any way. It is like watching TV, only in your mind. How easy can this be?

As you watch your word, your mind may shift to other thoughts or you may start listening to sounds coming from around you. You may forget that you are doing the Gate Technique for a while. You may lose yourself in thoughts, sometimes for minutes at a time. No biggie. If this happens, when you realize you are not observing your word, just serenely find it again. That's it! The power of the Gate Technique is in its simplicity and innocence.

Now, one last thing, you may notice that your word occasionally disappears. That's okay. Just observe the space it left behind. You will recognize it as the gap where pure awareness abides. The gap is not a goal. It is only another of the many changes your mind will go through. Soon, all by itself, your word will return. Or it may turn into another word. That is okay, too. Just accept the new word and watch or listen to it as you did the old one.

So, to review, sit quietly with your eyes closed. After a few

The power of the Gate Technique is in its simplicity and innocence.

seconds, easily find your word and simply observe what happens. Don't interfere, just watch. When you realize other thoughts or noises are there, quietly find your word and begin observing again. If you lose your word it will return or another will take its place. Just follow along.

It doesn't matter what happens as long as you purely observe, uninvolved, what is unfolding before you. Continue the Gate Technique for 10 to 20 minutes. (Always get in at least 10 minutes if you can.) When finished, do not open your eyes quickly or jump up and start doing things right away. Keep your eyes closed. Take another minute or two to stretch and come back to the outside world slowly. If you come out too quickly you may feel some irritability, headache or other physical discomfort. Whether you notice it or not, your body will be very relaxed and it needs time to transition to full activity. Your mind will want to get going, but give your body a chance to catch up. Then slide easily back into your active life. Do the Gate Technique at least once every day. However, twice a day quadruples its effects. The best time is as soon as you are awake. Your second experience is fine sometime later during your day. If you can't squeeze it in during the day, do it before bed. This will blissfully dissolve the day's stresses and make for a great night's sleep.

This is important for continued success. Reread these instructions, or listen to the Gate Technique download every couple of days in the beginning. This will erase any bad habits that may inadvertently work their way into the practice. It is common to think you are doing it correctly only to find that you have left something out or added something unnecessary. If you are not careful to maintain innocent observation, the Gate Technique will not be as effective and you will find yourself thinking that it is not working as well as it did in the beginning. This is a dead giveaway that some impurity has crept into your practice. After two weeks of checking your practice every couple of days, reread or play the instructions every two weeks. This will insure that you benefit fully from your practice.

The Gate Technique teaches us to rely on nothing other than observation. What happens is quite magical. A deep healing begins without a glimmer of effort. Actually, effort of any kind is counterproductive. What the Gate Technique effectively does is bathe your psyche in the healing waters of awareness. We are actually aligning with the wisdom that made the body/mind. When done regularly, you will experience greater energy, physically and psychologically, more relaxation, less illness, more resistance to mental and emotional stress, and improved relationships. All this is accomplished by simply paying attention. Very quickly you will notice that you are observing more and more outside of the Gate Technique during daily activities. The Gate Technique is prefect by itself or can be added to the beginning of other practices to enhance their effectiveness. Just be sure to not change the Gate Technique itself. Its power is in its simplicity. It is complete as it is. Adding to or removing anything from it will only make it less effective.

Soon you will be learning Quantum Entrainment, the scien-

A deep healing begins without a glimmer of effort...
All this is accomplished by simply paying attention.

tific method of instant healing. While the Gate Technique is not used directly in the Quantum Entrainment process, it does help to rarefy awareness which is the cornerstone of QE. Done daily it will quickly establish the habit of present awareness in activity. Later, when you are proficient with Quantum Entrainment, you can substitute QE for the Gate Technique, although many people continue to do both. Now it is time to look at what Quantum Entrainment is and how it works. Then you will learn how to actually heal with QE.

Chapter Eight

Quantum Entrainment

"God doesn't look at how much we do, but with how much love we do it."
- Mother Teresa -

"Intuition is the source of scientific knowledge."
- Aristotle -

W hat is Quantum Entrainment? *Quantum Entrainment is a quick and effective scientific method that reduces pain and promotes healing. It creates immediate changes that can be seen and felt in the body. It is reproducible and will stand up to the scientific rigor of pre- and post-testing. QE continues to work long after the initial session, gently balancing and eliminating blocks to physical and emotional well-being. It enlivens a healing awareness in both the initiator and the receiver of the process. There is generally a feeling of peace and relaxation that accompanies a QE session.*

Quantum Entrainment wakes us up to our own inner awareness. When we become more familiar with pure awareness we feel better in every way. When we become healthier and happier, it is only natural that we want to share it with others. Soon we will learn the Quantum Entrainment method of instant healing. Then the cycle will be complete. You will have learned to give what you get. Or more accurately, you will learn to share what you are. As it turns out, the people you share your awareness with are also pure awareness. You will simply be awakening them to their basic nature. I would like to expand on this fascinating concept here but this is a journey that would take us well beyond the covers of this book. If you would like to know more about your inner basic nature as it relates to health, relationships and happiness, I recommend you pick up a copy of Beyond Happiness: How You Can Fulfill Your Deepest Desire by this author. It makes pretty interesting reading if I do say so myself. Okay, okay, let's get back on track and leave this shameless self-promotion behind.

Quantum Entrainment wakes us up to our own inner awareness.

Pure awareness, we will soon discover, is a powerful regenerator of things gone wrong. Symptoms such as pain, confusion and depression tell us something is amiss. Symptoms are signposts pointing toward a breakdown in order within the body/mind. Whether it is a broken leg or a broken heart, disorder runs counter to a smoothly functioning, productive and loving body/mind.

Health is order. The more order we reflect the healthier we are. When health begins to break down we have a multitude of medicines and therapies aimed at reestablishing that order in our body/mind.

We can simplify the question of health by looking at it from a vibrational point of view. A vibration, or wave, is the simplest expression of energy. Stars and frogs, angels and anvils are nothing more than conglomerates of energy waves which coalesce to create those very forms.

Pure awareness is a powerful regenerator of things gone wrong.

Health is order. The more order we reflect the healthier we are.

We can look at our organs and tissues, thoughts and emotions as individual bundles of vibrations that work in sympathy to create a healthy body/mind. When vibrations get out of sync we call it a disorder or a disease, then try to heal it. Most healing is accomplished by introducing orderly vibrations to neutralize the disorderly ones. For instance, the herbal vibration white willow bark will neutralize the inflammation vibration of a headache.

The process of strengthening or weakening vibrations is called interference. I think the simplest way to look at it is this. Amplitude is the vertical part of a wave, how high it is. If you add two waves of the same amplitude together you end up with one big wave twice the amplitude of the original. (*Figure 4: Wave Interference.*) This is called constructive interference. The opposite is also true. If you add two waves of exactly opposite amplitude, they cancel each other out and you end up with zero amplitude. This is called destructive interference.

Don't let all this constructive/destructive interference jargon boggle your inner workings. Go down to the sea shore and watch the waves roll in and you will see this principle at work. As you watch, you will soon see that a faster wave will overtake the slower one in front of it. The two merge and make a single stronger wave. The momentum of that bigger, faster moving wave pushes it farther up the beach than the other waves, soak-

Figure 4:
Wave Interference

Constructive Interference

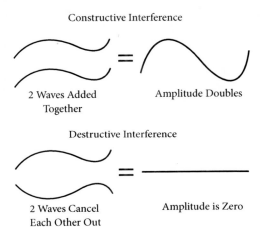

2 Waves Added
Together

Amplitude Doubles

Destructive Interference

2 Waves Cancel
Each Other Out

Amplitude is Zero

ing your brand new wingtip tennies. That is constructive inter-ference.

As that wave washes back down the beach, leaving your feet submerged to the ankles in a pool of sandy sea water while you stream blue expletives effectually from behind clenched teeth and mothers up and down the beach sprint frantically to cover their babies' ears, it meets another wave coming in. The force of the outgoing wave reduces the force of the incoming wave, which loses size and momentum and falls far short of where you were standing. Not that you would notice for you are already halfway back to your car, grumbling and sloshing sea water over the tops of your tennies with each step. The loss of momentum by the second wave is an example of destructive interference.

Traditional healing systems like medicine, acupuncture, body work and subtle energy procedures ultimately work by reestablishing vibrational order. The closer the treatment vibration matches the vibration of the healthy condition, the more complete the healing. Sometimes, disorder can actually be created by the treatment itself. If the treatment only partially matches the cure, as is the case with prescribed medications, side effects are created. Generally speaking, the closer the healing system is to working purely with waves or vibrations, the less chance of creating side effects. And that brings us back to pure awareness.

Pure awareness is not a vibration but the source of vibration. It is the potential order and energy behind every form. In theory, if we were somehow able to infuse pure awareness into a disorderly system, perfect order would result without side effects. As it so happens, it is possible! That system we call Quantum Entrainment.

Every healing method, system or procedure is meant to provide direction and support guiding the practitioner over possible hurdles that might prevent him or her from successfully completing the task at hand. We mistakenly think that it is the procedure that is responsible for success. It is not!

> *Pure awareness is not a vibration but the source of vibration.*
> *It is the potential order and energy behind every form.*

I am going to let you in on another secret; this one is on the house. It is not the healing procedure, but awareness that does the healing. That's right, awareness is the magic ingredient in every successful endeavor. It doesn't matter if you are washing the car, working a trigonometry problem or clipping your toenails, awareness is always the key ingredient. Just try and clip your toenails without it. Not a pretty picture.

It is not the healing procedure, but awareness that does the healing.

It is your awareness that breathes life into what you do. Technique by itself is lifeless. Awareness is like the train and the procedure is like the tracks. No awareness, no movement. Nothing gets done without awareness. That is why you can pick from any one of thousands of healing forms and still get well.

The Quantum Entrainment procedure puts the emphasis on awareness instead of the procedure. As you will soon experience, the actual technique is almost effortless. In fact, QE really starts working when the procedure stops. That's right, when all the structure of the QE technique falls away into pure awareness that is when the healing takes place. You see, the QE procedure is not a healing technique. It is a process to become aware of pure awareness. Healing is actually a side effect of becoming aware. That also means that you are not the healer, pure awareness is. This is an important distinction that will become more apparent as you take up the practice of Quantum Entrainment.

Healing is actually a side effect of becoming aware.

It also brings up a vital point that needs looking at. If you are not the healer then you cannot take credit for any healing that gets done. You are free from that responsibility, free from that burden.

Let's say that you are asked to help relieve a very painful knee. You do not have to know if the knee is arthritic or sprained or anything else about it. You do not need to diagnose the problem. The infinite orderliness of awareness will do that for you. You do not need to know anything about the knee. You only need know what the owner of the knee wants, in this case, to remove the pain.

You only need to start the Quantum Entrainment process and the rest is taken care of for you. Actually not for you, for the person who has the pain. Other than the initial setup, nothing is done by or for you.

Before a QE session, which might last from 15 seconds to several minutes, you will learn how to perform a simple pre-test to note objectively the intensity of pain, swelling and other symptoms. After the session you will perform the same test and observe to what degree those symptoms have been relieved. Because you were not involved in the healing of the knee you should not have a vested interest in how or to what degree healing has taken place. This saves your psychology from bruising and keeps a leash on your ego. It also allows compassion and the joy of being human to fully blossom. Not bad dividends for a few minutes work, would you say?

You only need to start the Quantum Entrainment process and the rest is taken care of for you.

Quantum Entrainment is simply a process that allows awareness to expand into pure awareness for purposes of healing. Once the initiator of the QE process becomes aware of pure awareness, the actual healing takes place instantly. Although the discordant elements of any illness or condition become integrated in an instantn the results may take some time to fully manifest. Quantum Entrainment will continue to work long after the session is performed. This is another reason why you shouldn't get too wrapped up in the initial results. Let's say that the painful knee was 80% improved after the initial QE session. Two minutes later it could be 90% improved and two days later the pain may be completely gone.

Once the initiator of the QE process becomes aware of pure awareness, the actual healing takes place instantly.

So whatever happens will happen for the best. It is impossible to do harm. The ancient guiding dictum of the healer, "Above all else, do no harm," does not apply to QE for two reasons: you are not healing and pure awareness can do no harm.

But you are not left out of it altogether. The beauty of the Quantum Entrainment experience is that it heals both the partner and the initiator. (Note: We will refer to the person receiving QE as the "partner" and the person who is performing QE as the "initiator.") By virtue of the QE process, the initiator easily slips into a sublime state of pure awareness and then allows the perfect harmony of that subtle ground state to recreate or reorganize matter without disorder. When done regularly, this state of inner awareness begins to be felt outwardly, organizing and healing our every thought, word and action. The experience is peaceful, uplifting and inspiring.

In the next few paragraphs I'm going to generally compare and contrast Quantum Entrainment to other healing systems. This is for your understanding. Please don't misunderstand my intentions. I am not commenting about the value of these methods. Every method of healing is precious and necessary. Just ask the millions whose quality of life is improved daily by their use. I am looking at a bigger picture of health, expanding it beyond the body and mind to encompass every realm of human interaction. We are truly limited by the conceptual chains that bind our minds and weaken our bodies.

> *Quantum Entrainment experience is that it heals*
> *both the partner and the initiator.*

You may only want to use Quantum Entrainment to heal a physical or emotional pain, and that is fine. More than just a method for healing body and mind, however, Quantum Entrainment flows easily outward to heal and enrich every human endeavor and beyond. And it all happens automatically. When QE is applied regularly, the sharp angles and hard surfaces of life soften. The result is that we come to know life as nurturing, a universal mother who protects and teaches and ultimately fulfills all our needs. This comes quickly when we rouse from our slumber to greet the new day with a sense of playfulness and awe. Quantum Entrainment is the first toy out of the toy box, and the last to be returned.

More than just a method for healing body and mind, however, Quantum Entrainment flows easily outward to heal and enrich every human endeavor...

When we play with QE daily, our personal ills begin to heal by themselves. Our healing is accelerated. We come to rely less and less on outside modalities and turn more easily inward to become a loving witness of life as it manifests through us. Like a snowball rolling downhill, we gather to us the fullness of life, increasing the momentum of health and vibrant living as we go.

But I am no purist and I don't think you should be either. Quantum Entrainment has the potential, and I stress the word potential, to be the magic bullet for problems of every sort. Daily, you will surprise yourself by performing little miracles. This experience will alter the basic foundation upon which you perceive this world. I mean come on, tapping into the creative source of the entire cosmos? I dare you to do that and maintain a business as usual attitude.

Daily, you will surprise yourself by performing little miracles.

What sets QE apart is that it does not rely on medicines, modalities, and mind sets. Where a traditional healing system embraces structure, QE looks to dissolve it. The orderly dissolution of structure opens the mind of the practitioner to pure awareness, which in turn adds order to structure.

All methods of healing have value. That value increases as the awareness of the practitioner increases. QE, like every other healing form, is limited by the mind of the practitioner. In a perfect world, Quantum Entrainment would be all we would need to assure ideal health and harmony in body, mind, relationships, job, spiritual pursuit, education and recreation. Yes, QE can restore harmony in all these areas. The bad news is Quantum Entrainment, like all healing procedures, is limited by the limitations of the practitioner. The good news is the practice of QE actually removes those limitations. Simply put, the more you practice Quantum Entrainment the more fun and fulfilling your life will be. Now let's turn our attention back to the nuts and bolts of Quantum Entrainment.

Quantum Entrainment is not a subtle energy procedure. QE does not employ wave interference or in any way try to neutralize abhorrent energy with herbs or medications, bodywork or manipulation, radiating energies, subtle energies or any other modality. Quantum Entrainment is unique in this respect and here's how.

> *The bad news is Quantum Entrainment, like all healing procedures, is limited by the limitations of the practitioner. The good news is the practice of QE actually removes those limitations.*

Any major system of healing, be it traditional medicine, subtle energy or anywhere in between, requires rigorous study and practice under the guidance of a qualified practitioner to safely and effectively apply it. More than likely, that system evolved over many years of trial and error before it was accepted as viable. Most healing systems are still evolving. They are as much an art as they are a science and results vary with the skill of the practitioner. All this caution and attention to detail is necessary because these systems can do harm if not properly applied. Or at the very least, they would be ineffective.

None of this applies to Quantum Entrainment for one simple reason. Ultimately the initiator doesn't do anything. S/he lets pure awareness do all the work. Remember, pure awareness is perfect order. If something appears to be disorderly pure awareness will fix it. The only thing we need the initiator for is to set the stage. S/he gets everything ready and then steps out of the way. Pure awareness then dissolves the disharmony and reassembles it in perfect working order while the initiator looks on in adjunct bliss.

How hard is it to learn Quantum Entrainment? It's as easy as thinking. The practice of Quantum Entrainment takes no special skills and can be learned quickly. In fact, it takes more effort to read about QE than to actually do it. So if you are reading this book you will be able to learn and apply QE. Then you will experience for yourself the phenomenal curative effects of pure awareness.

What is Quantum Entrainment good for? If you can think it, QE can fix it. It can fix it but that is not to say it will. Anything that pure awareness made, which just happens to be everything, pure awareness can fix. That makes sense, doesn't it? The thing is, pure awareness is what does the fixing, not us. It is not hampered by our personal needs, aspirations, prejudices, hopes, fears, goals, failures or anything else bouncing around inside our craniums. We humans see an incredibly tiny sliver of what is, has been, or will be. Our problem is that we think we have a pretty good idea of what is best in any given situation. The truth is we haven't a clue. At any given moment, our world is a seething sea of cause and effect. Every present cause is the result of infinite and interrelated effects reaching back countless eons to that first gentle thought that spawned the wellspring of creation. How is it possible to know the primal imputes that caused the thought we are thinking this very moment? Do you know what made you think that thought, or the thought before that one?

It takes more effort to read about QE than to actually do it.
If you can think it, QE can fix it.

Is it so hard to imagine that we are not the masters of our fate that we think we are? Consider a lifelong bachelor who, as a young man, was a minute late leaving for the grocery store because he misplaced his car keys. He arrived at the store a minute late and just missed meeting the only woman he could have ever loved. One minute, one second, can change a lifetime. We have all speculated at one time or another how our lives would have been different if we had bought one more lottery ticket or had not gone against our parents' wishes and became a street mime. Isn't every moment of our lives filled with forces beyond our control that could completely alter our future?

Let's take a break and play with a little abstraction, okay? Stretching the boundaries of our minds is always good and is especially useful when exploring new healing paradigms. If nothing else it will give our minds something to chew on. Like a seed, it could sprout and grow into something useful and ultimately quite magnificent.

Our world is a seething sea of cause and effect...
One minute, one second, can change a lifetime.

Quantum physics has exposed several viable theories of multiple universes. One I subscribe to is that every one of us has an infinite number of lives. It is not theory but a mathematical fact that time does not flow. It does not exist as we normally think of it. Our minds create the sequencing that we identify as time. In other words, time is a human creation that does not exist outside our minds. It is only our limited consciousness that confines us to one time and one life.

Time is a human creation that does not exist outside our minds.

It is a strong possibility that you exist in a parallel life just as you are with the exception of one minor change. For instance, in one life you might have arthritis in your fingers. In another you might have arthritis in your fingers and knees. In a third you might have no arthritis at all. Think about it, infinite expressions of you existing side by side. Wouldn't it be amazing if you could consciously move from one life to another? Your experience of life would be infinitely expanded, limited only by your consciousness. And now we are coming to a very interesting point.

What connects these multiple universes together? If each of your lives were a pearl on a necklace, what would be the thread that held them together? The unifying thread of multiple universes is Bohm's unbounded whole, the implicate order of pure awareness. Pure awareness is the portal to each of your lives. This may be how Quantum Entrainment works, by moving your consciousness through the portal of pure awareness to a parallel life. If you have arthritis in this life you effortlessly plunge into pure awareness and come back out free of arthritis in another.

That reminds me of one of the books in the *Chronicles of Narnia* written by C.S. Lewis where his characters could dive into a pond in England and surface in the world of Narnia. It seems that Lewis was intuiting what quantum physics is calling multiple universes.

I like to see it more like a music CD. Each track on the surface of the disc would represent a life. The laser light that reads the information sweeps along the CD releasing the music of each life locked within those tracks. The laser light is like our consciousness sweeping along the track we call our present life. Our consciousness moves from birth to death. But remember, there is no motion in time. This is fact. Time is an illusion created by our conscious mind. All our lives exist simultaneously just like all the tracks exist at one time on the CD. Now, what if, instead of the laser light moving predictably along one track after another, we could make it skip to a parallel track? We could start playing the parallel track, couldn't we? The instantaneous healing of an entire illness seems like magic until you realize that you just dived into pure awareness from one life and surfaced in another, free of that limiting disease.

I bring this up for a very good reason. The wonders that we can perform are limited only by our consciousness. We are all limited, every one of us. It is unavoidable. But knowing what we now know, we can begin to slip the chains that bind our consciousness and begin to live beyond our present limitations. Could curing our arthritis be as simple as switching tracks on a CD? Yes, if you know how and your mind will allow it. Built within the simple process of Quantum Entrainment are the mechanics of creation, the ability to open our awareness to the infinite possibilities that creation has laid before us.

The wonders that we can perform are limited only by our consciousness.

Now, theory is fun to play around with, and it has the potential to expand our minds beyond their present parameters. But the fact is, Quantum Entrainment works whether you have a theory or not. Quantum Entrainment works whether you believe in it or not. QE works even if you don't understand how it works. A child can perform Quantum Entrainment with perfect innocence. In fact, it will not work without it.

We can not create this shift in pure healing consciousness through sheer force of will. We can only place our innocent intention in the ocean of pure awareness. Where the currents of harmony and healing lead is beyond our influence. We can have a desire to heal someone but that desire comes from the limited us, awash in the ever-turbulent ocean of the mind. It may be an altruistic desire born of compassion for a suffering being. But there is no way we can know how the cosmic blueprint will support that desire. We cannot know what infinite, convoluted course of events has led to this apparent disharmony. Nor can we know in what way it will choose to express harmony once again. When Quantum Entrainment is performed there is always a change in the condition. It is possible that a single QE session can set in motion forces that will reverberate throughout the universe before that harmony is realized. As an initiator, all we can do is express our desire to make it right. The result, in whatever form it takes, will be a natural and perfect expression of pure awareness. We simply accept what we see with the knowledge that we cannot possibly know what forces are at work or when they will manifest.

A child can perform Quantum Entrainment with perfect innocence.
In fact, it will not work without it.

I once had a client who asked me to help her with several problems all at once. She had a sinus headache, upper shoulder muscle spasm from her work and was anemic from six weeks of pre-menopausal complications. I initiated the QE process for several minutes after which I noted some slight indication that her body had received the organizing influence of pure awareness. When I asked her how she felt she said that she felt exactly the same as before her session. I told her that the process was successful and that I could do no more for her now. I could see the disappointment on her face as she turned to leave. About an hour later I got an excited call from my client. She told me that while driving home the flood gates on her sinuses burst open and she almost had to stop the car to tend to her now freely flowing sinuses. She said that after she had been in her home for about 20 minutes her shoulders relaxed and she felt light and unburdened. I congratulated her and thanked her for taking the time to keep me updated on her condition. The next morning she called again, more excited this time. She told me she was completely free of any pre-menopausal symptoms.

It is possible that a single QE session can set in motion forces that will reverberate throughout the universe...

At the time QE was applied, this client had no outward indication that it had worked. I was aware of only the slightest change in a single muscle in her upper back. I didn't know what relief, if any, she would experience. I was saved from all that because I was more like a bystander to the process. I initiated Quantum Entrainment and stepped out of the way. I took great joy in the relief of her symptoms, not because I did something, but for another reason. Every time healing occurs in this way it is testimony that life is vaster than thought and more bounteous than imagination. When I initiate the QE process, I touch something that is greater than me and I come to know it as my Self. I come to have a feeling that is not hope, really, but a knowing that everything is right with my world. I don't perform QE just to make my life better. I do it to remind me that perfection already is, to make ripples on the pond of immortality and watch as they playfully lap against the lives of my fellow travelers in this infinitesimally small slice of the universe.

Chapter Nine

Preparing to Heal

"The soul never thinks without a mental picture."
- Aristotle -

"Think left and think right and think low and think high.
Oh, the thinks you can think up if only you try!"
- Dr. Seuss -

Preparing to apply Quantum Entrainment is not so much a gathering of tools and technique as it is a preparation to do nothing. Those who know me well are not surprised that I discovered and developed Quantum Entrainment. They are quick to point out that I have been preparing to do nothing most of my life. It's nice to have such observant and supportive friends.

The first thing I would like is for you to demonstrate to yourself the power of awareness by creating an observable change in your body. By performing this striking exercise you will not only get the simple basics for healing but you will get a little taste of the joy and delight of healing Quantum Entrainment style. Ready? Let's get started.

Preparing to apply Quantum Entrainment is not so much a gathering of tools and technique as it is a preparation to do nothing.

Experience Three: The Growing Finger Exercise

Hold up your hand, palm facing you, and find the horizontal line, or crease, that runs along the bottom of your hand at the top of your wrist. Find the same horizontal crease on your other hand. Place your wrists together so that the two creases lineup exactly with each other. Now, carefully bring your palms and fingers together. Your hands should line up perfectly in prayer-like fashion.

Look at how your two middle fingers line up. They will either be even in length or one will be shorter than the other. For this exercise you will pick the shorter finger. If your fingers are even, you get to choose either the right or the left one.

Separate your hands and place them on the table or in your lap. Look at the middle finger you chose and think, "This finger will grow longer." Now, don't move the finger. Just become acutely aware of it. You can do this with you eyes open or closed, it does not matter. Look at the finger or envision it in your mind. Focus all your awareness on that single finger; that is all. Do this for one full minute. You don't have to tell it again to grow longer. Once is enough. Just provide what it needs to make the transition, *focused awareness*. That one finger gets your total attention for one full minute.

After one minute has passed, again measure the length of your fingers using the creases across your wrists exactly as you did before. Note the lengths of your two middle fingers, and presto change-o! the finger that received your awareness will be longer. That is pretty amazing when you stop to think about it. (Yes, pun intended.) Welcome to the wonderful world of heightened awareness. You've just witnessed how the force of awareness can animate the body and prepare it for healing from within. But how were you were able to perform this magical feat (should I say, magical finger)? Let's find out.

The basics for this exercise were intention and awareness. First, you had the single intention for your short finger to grow longer. Then you focused all your awareness on that finger. This exercise gets us in the neighborhood of Quantum Entrainment but we are not quite there. We only need add one additional element, the Eufeeling, and you will be ready to become a healing dynamo.

Chapter Ten

Feelings and Eufeelings

"Peace is a butterfly, which, when pursued, is always just beyond your grasp, but which, if you will sit down quietly, may alight upon you."
- Nathaniel Hawthorne -

What is the difference between anger, pride, worry, sorrow and other feelings and the Eufeelings of peace, joy and bliss? Simply put, feelings are conditional and Eufeelings are not. Feelings are created by other feelings, thoughts and circumstances. Eufeelings arise directly out of pure awareness. When you get angry you do so for a reason. For instance you may be angry with your spouse for leaving the cap off the tube of toothpaste. You may be sad because someone close to you has left. You may be worried because you can't pay the bills. There are conditions for all feelings whether we are aware of them or not.

Eufeelings (short for euphoric feelings) are unconditional feelings. They do not have or need a reason for being. They just are. For instance, peace exists wherever we are at all times. Once you know how, you can find peace, like the eye of the storm, even in the middle of an emotional hurricane. When you are Self-aware, aware of pure awareness, you will experience peace along with whatever else you are thinking or doing. You may even recognize that it has been there all along but you haven't been paying attention to it. Peace is your natural state of being when you are not caught in the emotional milieu of everyday conditional feelings. If you are unfamiliar with pure awareness you may find this last statement hard to believe. You won't after learning Quantum Entrainment. The QE process naturally and easily brings your everyday awareness to pure awareness and the Eufeelings that shimmer in the subtlest reaches just beyond your mind.

Eufeelings arise directly out of pure awareness.

Conditional feelings are creations of the mind and caught in time. They serve the needs of the ego to divide and conquer. All conditional feelings have opposites, for instance happiness has sadness and love has isolation. And they are always associated with the past or the future. Eufeelings have no opposites. They are ethereal melodies of pure awareness gently lapping the remote shores of our minds. Always singing but seldom heeded, they are the first and faint articulations of the eternity that we are.

The primal Eufeeling peace can also be known as silence or stillness, joy, bliss or unconditional love, ecstasy and the experience of the awe of oneness. Any one Eufeeling contains within it all Eufeelings. In peace is stillness. If you are observant you will find peace to be joyful. If you are especially quiet you will find the innocence of unbounded love there too, ready to enfold you in its subtle embrace.

While Eufeelings stand on their own they can produce conditional feelings in the mind. For instance, when you experience pure joy it may arouse feelings of pleasure or happiness in the mind. The Eufeeling from the cusp of the mind is perceived as happiness in the mind. In this case the conditional feeling "happiness" still needed a reason for being. That reason was the Eufeeling joy. Conditional feelings like anger and lust produce other conditional feelings. But conditional feelings can never produce Eufeelings.

Once you know how, you can find peace, like the eye of the storm, even in the middle of an emotional hurricane.

This is a very important point to ponder. We must discriminate between feelings generated in the mind to appease the ego's need for dissension and the Eufeelings that support infinite harmony and peace. If we do not, we will remain chained to the whirling wheel of emotional turbulence that has brought our world to the threshold of annihilation. Once understood it is easy enough to remedy. Experience first the universal harmony of peace, joy and love and let the healing unfold spontaneously from within.

If the mind were a light bulb then pure awareness would be the electricity that makes it light up. Eufeelings would be the light that is produced by the electricity moving through the filament. Conditional feelings would be alterations in the glass of the bulb, like color or printing (60 W) or distortions like bubbles or wrinkles. To carry the analogy a little further, if you were feeling a little depressed your bulb might be blue, angry might be red and so on. Even when the glass of the bulb is blue the light in the bulb is still pure and clear. It doesn't radiate blueness until it passes through the blue glass of the bulb. Eufeelings are always clear and pure, and even when we are depressed or angry Eufeelings are still present. If we identify with our "blueness" we miss the purity of the peace that resides always inside.

If the mind were a light bulb then pure awareness
would be the electricity that makes it light up.

Not to stretch this analogy too far, but we can use it to make another important point. When we see people who are depressed, angry, irritable, obnoxious, etc; we tend to focus on the color they are radiating. We focus on the emotion and miss the purity behind it. When we perform Quantum Entrainment, as part of the process we become aware of Eufeelings. They add momentum to the healing. As we continue with the practice of QE, over time we become more familiar with the primary purity before the thought or action is performed. This knowing quickly spills over into our daily life and we begin spontaneously to recognize the peace, joy and unbounded love behind the behavior.

Because we know pure awareness in ourselves and recognize it in others, we are less influenced by another's negative behavior. This leaves us free to enjoy whatever Eufeeling happens to be reflecting in our mind at the time, be it peace, joy, bliss or unbounded love. We not only become more tolerant and loving toward others but ourselves as well. Accepting our own apparent imperfections and the behavior they spawn is a wonderful freedom and the foundation for living every day in peace.

Chapter Eleven

The Three P's of the QE Intention

"He who chooses the beginning of a road chooses the place it leads to."
- Harry Emerson Fosdick -

The main ingredient, as it were, of QE is pure awareness. As pure awareness reflects in your mind it creates the second ingredient, a Eufeeling. There is one more component of QE we need to discuss to complete the Three-Steps of Quantum Entrainment. That final component is the intention.

Intention gives direction to pure awareness. It informs the formless what form we want it to take. When you get a meal at a drive-thru restaurant, you put in your order at a menu board, make the short drive to the service window and then pick up your order. What goes on inside the restaurant really doesn't concern you. QE is a lot like ordering a happy meal. You simply place your healing order, take a little trip through pure awareness, and the results are waiting for you when you arrive at the window of life. Corny, yes, but I think it gets the idea across. Intention is the part where you place your order. How simple can this be?

Intention gives direction to pure awareness.

There are all kinds of intentions in this world. Some are simple and some are really convoluted, right down to the 10th decimal place. For our purposes, simple is better. The QE intention has three parts. Each one starts with a "P" so it's even that much easier to remember.

The three P's of the Quantum Entrainment intention are:

- Present
- Precise
- Positive

"Present" means right now. "Precise" means you identify clearly what it is you are healing, and "positive" means you approach the condition as if it were already healed. A negative intention would take up a position against something like eliminating pain or fighting cancer cells. There is no need for negative intention with the QE process. In fact, it is counter productive.

We are not fighting a battle against pain or anything else. Pain is not an enemy but an aberration. Pain is like a misbehaving child that needs love and direction. The QE intention is more like an invitation. It is an invitation for pure awareness to be the honored guest of our body/mind homes. And in return pure awareness loves our misbehaving pains and problems. All disharmony eventually dissolves in the loving embrace of pure awareness.

QE is a lot like ordering a happy meal.

Let's take a look at a Quantum Entrainment intention. If you want a sprained ankle to heal your intention might be: *"A normally functioning ankle, free of pain and swelling."* First note how simple and to the point this intention is. This is all we need. This simple intention is enough to give pure awareness the framework within which to heal. This intention identifies the ankle (precise) as if it were at this very moment (present) healed (positive). As you will discover, you only need focus on the finished product and awareness will do all the work. This really is the lazy person's guide to healing. Now let's move on to the final and most vital ingredient in the QE Three-Step healing process, pure awareness.

Chapter Twelve

Finding Pure Awareness

"Awareness is primordial; it is the original state, beginningless,
endless, uncaused, unsupported, without parts, without change."
- Nisargadatta -

"Awareness isn't selective. It's the absolute space in which everything happens."
- Karl Renz -

The reason Quantum Entrainment is so simple and yet so remarkably effective is because it draws on the infinite healing orderliness of pure awareness. It stands to reason that the initiator of the QE process should know what pure awareness is and how to contact it, or, more accurately, become aware of it. Pure awareness has gotten a good deal of press over the years. Mostly people who have written about it tell us that it is very hard to attain. They say it takes years of study and practice to get a handle on pure awareness. I say it is impossible to attain and you will never get a handle on it. That is because you already have it. You can't get something you already have. It's not hard, it's impossible. This is probably why so many of us have had such difficulty realizing pure awareness. We believe it is something that can be figured out, something that can be grasped with the mind. But, because pure awareness is essentially nothing, we cannot grasp it with either the hand or the mind. We can't even experience it. And this is an important point, too.

You can't get something you already have. It's not hard, it's impossible.

Pure awareness can only be known by the lack of experience. You know, like when you discovered the gap between your thoughts. It was a lack of experience that you realized only after you started thinking again. Pardon my grammar but the mind doesn't like "nothing." It wants to play with ideas or anything else that attracts its attention. That's why it makes finding pure awareness so hard. It has to. The mind can't know "nothing" so it has to make a philosophy to define it and a complicated technique to find it. Then it revels in conditional feelings, like self-satisfaction and pride, in an effort to convince itself that it was successful. All doomed to failure.

Pure awareness can't be realized by working at it. It can be realized by not working at it. The trick is to keep the mind busy with something else and then point out that awareness was there all along. We did this when we found the gap between thoughts. We're going to do this again, but when we finish you will be able to recognize pure awareness instantly, whenever you want.

Pure awareness can't be realized by working at it.
It can be realized by not working at it.

The process we will employ is very effective, but somewhat lengthier than the simple "Stopping Thoughts" exercise you did in Chapter 5. You will need to find a comfortable chair where you won't be interrupted for at least 20 minutes. Do not do this exercise lying down the first few times. The mind is more alert when the body is vertical.

There are several ways to do the Pure Awareness Technique. I have arranged for you to download it free from my website at: *www.QuantumEntrainment.org (your passoword is qe31).* It is in MP3 format so you can listen to it on your computer, MP3 player or make a CD. Your second choice is to read the text below into a recorder and play it back when you are ready for the experience. A third way to go through this process is to have someone else read it to you. There should be no communication between you and your reader once she begins to read. At the end of the reading, silence should be maintained for two or three minutes before opening your eyes. At that point, do not communicate with your reader until after you are aware of pure awareness with your eyes open. Finally, as a last resort, you can read the instructions through a couple of times and do the exercise from memory. This will work well but may take several attempts for you to realize pure awareness spontaneously.

Not to worry, I am here for you. If you have any questions or concerns, you can reach me through the "contact Frank" page at *www.QuantumEntrainment.org.* While you are visiting, drop by the QE Blog. The link will be found on the homepage of the QE website. There you will find information and comments by other QE'ers and can even enter your own thoughts for all to share in. One way or another you will quickly come to know pure awareness. In all likelihood you will need no more help than what you find between the covers of this book. But if you want more guidance, I am at your service. Now let's get to the business of finding pure awareness.

Experience 4: The Pure Awareness Technique

Sit comfortably in your chair with your hands separated. Close your eyes and become aware of your right hand. Do not move your hand. Just be aware of it. Pay close attention to what you feel in your right hand. See if you can feel your pulse or any muscle tension. Do you feel any discomfort or pain? Can you become aware of a generalized feeling like heat or cold, relaxation or tingling?

- (Do this for 30 seconds)
- Now become aware of your left hand in the same way.
- (15 seconds)
- Then become aware of both hands at the same time.
- (10 seconds)
- Become simultaneously aware of both wrists.
- (Only 2-3 seconds are needed for each body part from here.)
- Both lower arms.
- Your elbows.
- Your upper arms.
- Your shoulders.
- Become simultaneously aware of your arms from your fingertips to your shoulders.
- Become aware of the area across your upper back.
- Now your middle and lower back.
- Your whole back.
- Your sides, from your armpits to your hips.
- Become aware of your chest.

- Your abdominal area.
- Your pelvis. Become aware of your whole pelvic region.
- Become aware of your hips.
- Your upper legs.
- Your knees.
- Your lower legs.
- Your ankles.
- Become aware of your heels.
- Your soles.
- The tops of your feet.
- Your toes.
- Become simultaneously aware of your big toes.
- Your second toes.
- Your third toes.
- Your fourth toes.
- Your little toes.
- Become aware of your legs, your arms and your torso.
- Now become aware of your neck.
- Your chin.
- Your jaw.
- Your right ear.
- Your left ear.
- Your lower lip.
- Your upper lip.
- Become aware of the line between your lips.
- Become aware or your right nostril.
- Your left nostril.

- The tip of your nose.
- Your whole nose.
- Become aware of your right eyelid.
- Your left eyelid.
- Your right eye.
- Your left eye.
- Your right eyebrow.
- Your left eyebrow.
- The space between your eyebrows. Become aware of the space between your eyebrows.
- Your forehead.
- The back of your head.
- The top of your head.
- Your whole head.
- Become aware of your whole body. Have awareness of your whole body.
- (10 seconds.)
- Now become aware of an area around your body, an area of about 12 inches around your body, like an oval or egg surrounding your body.
- (10 seconds.)
- Now let your awareness expand further away from your body.
- (5-6 seconds. From here, we should hold each object in the mind for 5 or 6 seconds.)
- Become aware of your awareness filling the whole room.
- Now expand beyond the room and become aware of your awareness in the whole building.

- Expanding above the building, become aware of an area around the building.
- Expanding ever more rapidly upward, become aware of the whole city.
- Expanding still more rapidly, become aware of the area around your city, the country and neighboring cities.
- The whole state and neighboring states.
- Become aware of all of North America.
- Of the whole western hemisphere.
- The whole earth. Become aware of the whole earth spinning silently, powerfully on its axis.
- Your awareness continuing to expand, the earth grows smaller and smaller, the moon a silver dot.
- The earth grows smaller and smaller until it is just a glistening light the size of a star in the sky.
- Your awareness continues to expand and the sun slips silently by.
- It becomes smaller and smaller until it is the size of the other stars in the sky.
- You become aware of the millions and billions and trillions of other stars filling the sky. All within your awareness.
- Your awareness continues to expand and the stars form into our galaxy, spiraling silently, powerfully on its axis.
- And still your awareness continues to expand and our galaxy gets smaller and smaller until it is the size of a star in the sky.

- It is lost amongst the millions and billions and trillions of other galaxies in the sky.
- As your awareness expands all the galaxies, all of creation takes the form of an oval or egg suspended and supported by your awareness.
- All of creation is contained in this single glistening cosmic egg within your awareness.
- As your awareness continues to expand the egg of creation grows smaller and smaller.
- It is the size of a grapefruit.
- The size of an orange.
- The size of a lemon.
- The size of a pea.
- The size of a single glistening star in the sky.
- As your awareness expands all of creation becomes the size of a brilliant pinprick of light suspended in your unbounded awareness.
- Then all of creation, that single pinprick of light, winks out.
- (30 seconds.)
- Now again become aware of your whole body.
- (15 seconds.)
- Become aware that you are sitting in this room filled with your awareness. Everything in the room is in your awareness.
- (15 seconds.)
- Become aware that all of creation is in your awareness.
- (15 seconds.)

- Become aware of your whole body again, sitting in your awareness.
- Now take 2-3 minutes sitting easily before you open your eyes. Maintain your expanded awareness as you begin to open your eyes.
- (1 minute)
- Don't be in a hurry. Take time to come out, easily aware of your awareness filling the whole room.
- (1 minute)
- With your eyes still closed, slowly wiggle your fingers and toes or stretch lightly. Be aware of your awareness permeating your body and filling the room.
- (30 seconds)
- Now slowly open your eyes while you are aware that your awareness fills the whole room.
- (10 – 15 seconds.)
- (With eyes open.) Are you still aware of your awareness filling the whole room? Look at any object. Are you aware of your awareness between you and the object? Your awareness has always been there. You are just becoming aware of it outside of yourself.
- How do you feel?
- (5-7 seconds.)
- Do you feel some peace or quietness? Some light-ness or bliss?
- (5-7 seconds.)
- The quiet easiness you feel is a Eufeeling. It is a

reflection in your mind of pure awareness. It doesn't matter if you feel it as joy or peace or stillness, it is the result of being aware of pure awareness.

- Are you aware of your awareness filling the room right now?
- (3-5 seconds)
- See, it is still there. It is always there and now you will always be aware of it whenever you want. Do it again. Become aware of your awareness in the whole room.
- (3-5 seconds.)
- Now become aware of your awareness in your whole body.
- (3-5 seconds.)
- It's there too! Pure awareness is everywhere. It's like the coat that you forget you are wearing. All you have to do is think about it and you will know it is there, always keeping you warm. Whenever you think about pure awareness, that is, become aware of it, you will find it waiting for you. Wherever you are, there it is. It's like the young child of a loving mother. When the child misses mother she only has to look around to see that mother is watching over her.
- Go ahead, is mother watching? Become aware of your awareness filling the whole room, your body, all of creation.
- (5-7 seconds.)
- That took no effort at all, did it? You didn't have

to do something to find awareness, did you? You just became aware that it is there. Now you don't need a technique to find pure awareness only to lose it again when you stop the technique. You will be aware of pure awareness forever and without effort. Now how cool is that!

- Okay, one more thing. Close your eyes again and become aware of your awareness filling the room.
- (15 seconds.)
- Now pay attention to what you are feeling, your Eufeeling. Just identify if you are feeling peace, or stillness, or quiet or bliss, etc., find your Eufeeling and watch it for awhile.
- (8-10 seconds.)
- Nice, isn't it? Now open your eyes. Become aware of awareness all around you and again identify your Eufeeling with your eyes open. It could be the same or different, doesn't matter. Just pay attention to what Eufeeling you are having right now.
- (8-10 seconds.)

In preparation for creating a healing event with Quantum Entrainment, I would like you to, every now and again throughout your day, become aware of pure awareness and the Eufeeling associated with it at that time. The first few times, you may need to start out in a quiet environment with your eyes closed. But after a couple of times you will be aware of your Eufeelings even in the middle of rush hour traffic. Remember to become aware of pure awareness first. Then while you are watching, or feeling pure awareness, your Eufeeling will effortlessly shine through. While becoming aware of awareness is effortless, it takes the mind a little time to get used to a good feeling that is not associated with some activity. The Eufeeling is the subtlest activity in the mind and it just takes a time or two to get your otherwise active mind used to hanging out on that quiet level.

Okay, that does it for now. Glad to have had you along for the ride. Now that you are among the newly awakened, fully savor your new awareness and the joy it will visit upon you.

Chapter Thirteen
How to Heal In Three-Steps

"Miracles do not happen in contradiction to nature, but only in contradiction to that which is known in nature."
- St. Augustine -

There are only two ways to live your life. One is as though nothing is a miracle. The other is as though everything is a miracle."
- Albert Einstein -

Healing with Quantum Entrainment is actually realizing that you are not healing. You are not creating positive energy to overcome negative energy. You are not calling on other forces or formulas to do your bidding. You are creating an atmosphere in which healing will take place. Quantum Entrainment is tapping into the field, for lack of a better word, of perfect order. From there you do nothing and everything gets done for you. As a matter of convention I will say "You heal" or "I healed," but that is not strictly true. In preparation for creating a healing event, we must adopt the correct angle of entry to be successful. For me to say that we do not perform the healing is neither attitude nor philosophy. It is simple fact based on observation. This healing presence is not a foreign force that is beyond you but your very own essence, pure awareness; nothing more, nothing less.

Quantum Entrainment is tapping into the field of perfect order.

76

You will be amazed at the power your awareness holds. But know that you do not own that power. You are that power. Soon you will experience it first hand. You will slip beyond the boundaries that you have meticulously built, these past decades, to define the little you. These boundaries have confined your awareness to thoughts and things that have all served to strengthen your concept of "me." That will all be set aside the very first time you experience Quantum Entrainment.

You will be amazed at the power your awareness holds.
But know that you do not own that power. You are that power.

Now let's roll up our sleeves and get ready to create a healing event. Let us start with a simple case. Let's say that a friend has asked you to help him with left shoulder pain and muscle tension in the upper back and neck. With QE it is not necessary to know the cause of the condition. Healing will take place on the causal level automatically. As the initiator of Quantum Entrainment you only need to know what is desired. Obviously your partner desires relief from the shoulder pain and muscle tension. That is inferred. That is also your intention. So the stated intention for this condition might be *free of left shoulder pain and tension in the upper back and neck.* Can you see the Three P's of intention, present, precise and positive, at work here? See how simple the intention is? That is all you need.

Getting Ready to Heal

Before you start, have your partner move his shoulder so it creates the pain he wants to remove. Have him show you how his range of motion is diminished and anything else that demonstrates how the body is affected by this condition. Then have him grade the severity of his problem 1-10, 10 being "unbearable," and note that number. Get into the habit of pre-testing and post-testing. This will give you valuable feedback, especially in the beginning when you are just getting used to the QE process. If you are a physician, use the same tests you would for traditional treatment. For instance, a chiropractor might use orthopedic and neurological tests, palpation and even X-rays to objectively identify the problem and determine improvement.

Get into the habit of pre-testing and post-testing.

Take a few seconds to clearly form the intention in your mind. In this case we'll use the intention "Free of left shoulder pain and tension in the upper back and neck." You only need to clearly think the intention one time. Pure awareness is not deaf. It will know what you want. Now we are ready to start.

Triangulation: The Three-Step QE Process

(*Figure 5: Triangulation Back of Partner.*) On your partner's shoulder, upper back or neck it should be easy to find a muscle that is tight or painful to the touch. Place the tip of your index finger (Contact A) on a tight muscle. Push in firmly so you can feel how hard or tense the muscle is. Then relax and let your finger rest lightly on the tight muscle. Now lightly place the index finger of your other hand (Contact B) on any another muscle. This muscle does not have to be taut or sore to the touch. Just pick a muscle at random and place your finger there.

Figure 5:
Trianguation

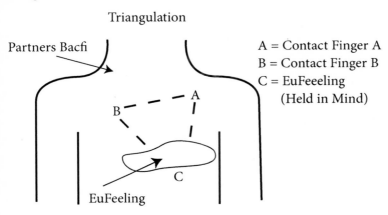

Triangulation

Partners Bacfi

A = Contact Finger A
B = Contact Finger B
C = EuFeeeling
(Held in Mind)

A

B

C

EuFeeling

Now focus all your attention on the first finger (Contact A) and become very aware of what you feel. Take time to notice the heat from his muscle on the tip of your finger, the texture of the skin or clothing, the tightness of the muscle pushing back against your finger, etc. Become aware of everything you can where finger and muscle meet.

Next, become acutely aware of the tip of the second finger (Contact B) just as you did with the first finger. Now become clearly aware of what both fingers are feeling *at the same time.* Maintain this awareness of both fingers for several seconds. Then, while you simultaneously hold your attention on both fingers, you will also notice a separate part of you that is just watching the whole process take place. You, your awareness, is aware of both fingers. So far, you have awareness of Contact A and awareness of Contact B and awareness that you are aware of both at the same time. It doesn't matter if you are clearly aware of this phenomenon or not, it is happening naturally, without effort.

As you hold awareness of the two points in this expanded way, do nothing. That's right, just pay attention to what you are sensing in the tips of your two fingers and that is all. If you are simultaneously paying attention to your two contact fingers and nothing else, you will soon begin to feel a sense of quietness or stillness or even peace. This is a Eufeeling generated from your expanded awareness. At this point, become aware of your Eufeeling while you hold your awareness on Contacts A and B.

You now have three points of awareness, Contact A, Contact B and your Eufeeling. Holding these three points in your awareness is called "triangulation." Continue to be aware of all three points until you feel a change in your partner's body, particularly in his muscles. (This can take several minutes when you are first learning QE.) The change you experience may be a softening or loosening of the muscles under your fingers. It may feel like your fingers are relaxing or dissolving into the muscles themselves. Or you may feel that your partner is generally relaxing. His shoulders might loosen or he may sigh or take a deeper breath. If you are standing, you might notice that your partner is swaying or his knees are buckling slightly.

All these changes are indicators that your partner's body is healing. It is reorganizing to eliminate the disorderly pain and tension. After you notice any of these indicators, continue to triangulate by holding your attention on the two contact points and your Eufeeling a little while longer. Then remove your fingers. Congratulations, you have just completed your first Quantum Entrainment session. With just two fingers and your

Eufeeling you have eliminated your partner's suffering!

What is your partner doing while you are creating this healing event? He is doing absolutely nothing. I am often asked by partners if they should relax or meditate or repeat their own intention. They should do nothing. They should not try to help in any way. If they do it can only slow down or counteract your efforts. The reason for this is, while their mind is busy with other chores it is less open to the healing influence QE generates. A mind in neutral will drop naturally and effortlessly into the healing waters of pure awareness.

Make your partners comfortable. If they like, they can close their eyes but that is all the preparation you need. If they want to help you in some way you can tell them that the best thing they can do is to let their mind wonder wherever it wants to go. Quantum Entrainment works very well under the most trying circumstances. Your partner may be in a great deal of physical or emotional pain. You may find yourself performing QE in an emergency room, a crowded mall or in any unsettling environment, and healing will still take place. So don't think you are limited by these things. But, given the choice, a settled environment with a compliant partner is always preferable.

The QE Session in a Nutshell

- Partner describes pain
- Pre-test
- Think intention
- Become aware of Contact A
  (hard or painful muscle)
- Become aware of Contact B

- Become aware of both A & B at same time
- Wait for Eufeeling
- Hold awareness of A & B & Eufeeling
- Muscle under Contact A relaxes
  (or other signs of relaxation)
- Post-test

Chapter Fourteen

What to Do After a QE Session

"This was love at first sight, love everlasting: a feeling unknown, unhoped for, unexpected - in so far as it could be a matter of conscious awareness; it took entire possession of him, and he understood, with joyous amazement, that this was for life."
- Thomas Mann -

Now let me ask you: When you finished your QE session, did you feel relaxed and peaceful? Quantum Entrainment heals the healer as well as the healed. Both you and your partner should be feeling quieter, a little more peaceful even beyond any excitement either of you may be having. Relaxation is the body's reaction to the healing presence of pure awareness. Peace is the reflection of pure awareness in the mind.

Make sure your partner is comfortable. The QE experience can be a little disorienting for some people. The sudden rush of pure awareness may take them away from this world for a bit. Afterward, they may need a little time for their mind and body to reorient to the here and now. If this happens it generally only lasts a few minutes. Give them their space until they are ready to resume.

Quantum Entrainment heals the healer as well as the healed.

On occasion, especially after an extended Quantum Entrainment session, your partner may need more time to adjust to her new body and she may become tired or so relaxed that she does not want to move. If at all possible under these circumstances, make sure your partner gets the rest she needs. This just means that great amounts of physical and emotional stresses are being released, and rest is the most expedient way for this transition to take place. After all, rest is the universal healer and pure awareness is the deepest rest possible. If your partner can't rest right then, suggest she gets to bed early that evening. She will awaken to a bright new world with extra bounce in her step.

Rest is the universal healer and pure awareness is the deepest rest possible.

The best time to do your post-test is as soon as you have finished the Quantum Entrainment session and your partner is stable. Have her do the same thing she did before the QE session and grade the condition from 1 – 10. For the case mentioned here, you will just have your partner put her shoulder through the same range of motion and grade the pain and muscle tightness as she did before. This is necessary feedback for you in the early stages of learning QE. It is also good for your partner to get a more objective view of the healing that took place in her body.

QE heals so quickly and easily that it appears that nothing has happened. The post-test is a real eye-opener for many partners. I never get tired of watching their faces as they perform the post-test and a pain or restriction they've had for 30 years is gone in 30 seconds.

QE heals so quickly and easily that it appears that nothing has happened.

QE always works but not always in the way you want. That is because pure awareness has the big picture and knows exactly how healing should take place. There is almost always a significant relief of symptoms immediately after a QE session. If the problem is not completely eliminated initially, then it will take a little more time for the body to adjust. The healing will continue to take place over the next day or so and can even be noticed weeks later. It is not uncommon for me to do QE on a workshop participant in the morning and only see a drop of several points on the post-test. Then, by the break the pain is completely gone. Even though the actual correction takes place instantly by pure awareness during triangulation, it may take additional time for the body to integrate those corrections physiologically. We'll spend more time on this later.

There is no rule that says that you can't turn right around and do QE again for the same condition. If you think it will help, repeat the session. Or better yet, do multiple applications during a single session. Just keep your A contact and move your B finger to different areas. Or you can move both fingers if you like. That entirely depends on what you feel is best to do.

Perform QE as many times as you like. You can do no harm. But let me caution you against thinking that more is better. It isn't. You should have in your mind that one short session will take care of the problem and go from there. A little later I will show you how to do Extended QE. But for now, let's keep it simple, very, very simple. Deal? Good.

For all intents and purposes you are done. But in the beginning while you are sharpening your QE skills, it doesn't hurt for you to ask your partner a few questions. Ask him how he felt during QE or if any other pains are gone along with the original complaint. Inquire after his emotional well-being. Actually, ask any questions you need to know to help you more fully understand the power and potential of QE.

Perform QE as many times as you like. You can do no harm.

The whole Quantum Entrainment process should be delightful. If you find yourself getting tangled up in the instruction, that is natural at first. The process is seamless but reading about it takes considerably more effort than actually doing it. Just relax into it and follow the instruction with a sense of adventure and play. Everyone can do QE. You are no different.

While Quantum Entrainment is simple and immediately effective, it is a new skill and you will need to practice it often in the beginning. Remember, well begun is half done. The more feedback you gather at this stage the more quickly you will become proficient at applying Quantum Entrainment. Practice QE on everyone, your friends, families, neighbors, even your pets. Soon you will learn Remote QE. That means that you don't even have to have your partner present. You can sit comfortably at home and create a healing event with your friends and family scattered all over the world.

The first several times you practice Quantum Entrainment, I suggest that you and your partner stand. The main reason for standing is that you will get more precise feedback from your partner. In particular, you will notice her swaying, a sign that pure awareness is working. You will also more easily notice if she takes a sudden deep breath, another indicator QE is working its magic. It is not as easy to notice these indicators when your partner is seated or lying down.

I would also recommend that you begin working on your partners' backs in the beginning, or at least where they cannot see you. Being out of the line of sight allows them to relax rather than watching you. It doesn't matter for the sake of their healing. Quantum Entrainment will work regardless of your partner's state of mind. It is more for your comfort and concentration. Some initiators are a little self-conscious in the beginning and can be distracted if their partner is watching their every move.

Quantum Entrainment will work regardless of your partner's state of mind.

Another practical point, you do not have to put your fingers on the area of complaint. You can touch anywhere on the body and heal any other area, including internal organs. I was at a book fair promoting *Beyond Happiness: How You Can Fulfill Your Deepest Desire* when a fellow author approached me. He said that he had heard that I did a kind of weird thing that got rid of pain. I asked him what was bothering him. We had been standing for some time and his arthritic knee had become inflamed and swollen. I pre-tested him simply by asking him to stand on the knee in a way that increased the pain. Then I had him sit on a box of books. I didn't want to bend way over to place my hands on his knee so I positioned my fingers on his shoulders. He immediately turned around and reminded me that it was his knee that was hurting. I assured him I was working on his knee. I formed the intention and began triangulation on his upper shoulder muscles. Less than a minute later I asked him to stand as he did before to test the knee. He did and -- I never get tired of this part -- his eyes opened wide as a sense of wonder lit up his face. Pain free, he returned to his stall to sell more books than I did. My fingers contacted his shoulders but the intention made sure it was his knee that received the healing.

Sometimes a pain or other symptoms will worsen before they get better. Just assure your partner that this is normal. At this time, the body needs to exacerbate the condition for a short period for it to heal. Continue to triangulate and the pain will subside quickly. On rare occasions the patient will become too uncomfortable to continue. At this point discontinue QE. Perhaps you might perform QE on another problem or just sit quietly. After a few minutes perform the post-test and see if the condition still exists. If so, do QE again. In all likelihood the pain will dissolve with no further issues.

One last thing: since you are not doing any healing, you cannot take any credit for the results. This is a very important point. If you do not take credit for the results, you cannot be attached to the results. Do you see where I'm going with this? If you are not attached to the results of your QE session then you are able to accept whatever results appear. Complete acceptance of the fruits of your QE labor, whether more or less than you expected, alleviates mental discord. A mind free of discord is capable of reflecting Eufeelings. And Eufeelings, as we all know, are necessary for healing to unfold.

If you are not attached to the results of your QE session then you are able to accept whatever results appear.

When you have a healing agenda you diminish your ability to create a healing event. For instance, let's say the local news station wanted to do a news brief on your ability to heal based on several remarkable successes. When they show up the reporter asks you to perform QE on her indigestion. Feeling that you had better perform admirably or this will be a very short interview, you develop a pretty prevalent case of performance anxiety. Not wanting to be embarrassed you take your A & B contacts and wait for your Eufeeling. You are preoccupied with trying to remove her discomfort and you are already thinking about what you will look like on the 6 o'clock news. Your Eufeeling couldn't blast its way into your consciousness with a cannon because you are trying to heal with your thoughts. When the Eufeeling is a no-show you begin pushing energy and repeating your intention like beating a drum. At this point you might as well get her a Tums With Calcium because your dyspeptic mind cannot offer her relief.

QE is a powerful adjunct to traditional healthcare practices.

It is far easier to start a QE session by letting your partner know that you do not know how much healing will result. You might tell him, "We will accept whatever we get." You should also mention that not everything will be immediately obvious and healing may continue for several days after the session. Finally, you may mention that improved results sometime require additional QE sessions.

Now that you know how to create a healing event I thought it would be prudent for me to give you some additional ideas that will help you broaden and deepen your healing experience. For instance, we have barely mentioned psychological healing and yet this is an area in which Quantum Entrainment really shines.

But before we start, maybe I should take this opportunity to mention the obvious. Quantum Entrainment can be used for any kind of healing and should always be performed, not instead of but in conjunction with qualified healthcare treatment. QE is a powerful adjunct to traditional healthcare practices. It can only enhance the efforts of other healing systems, increasing the depth of healing and considerably shortening total healing time. Many times, if QE is done before seeing the appropriate healthcare practitioner the symptoms will disappear. Even if symptoms abate, one should always consult professional help to be certain there are no underlying etiologies or additional undiscovered problems.

The more you practice QE the more healing will take place in your own life. Your growing familiarity with pure awareness will spill over into your everyday life, bringing a level of fulfillment undreamed of. Equipped with nothing more than your own awareness, no matter where you go you can initiate a healing event. In essence, you are learning to love. Actually, you cannot learn to love, you are love. Eternal joy and unbounded love cannot be created. They are already there; otherwise they wouldn't be eternal and unbounded. They are waiting to be discovered by us. Pure awareness is pure love. Being aware is unconditional love in motion. We have heard that love conquers all. Now we have the opportunity to prove it. As you continue to initiate Quantum Entrainment you will luxuriate in the joy of helping others and receive their gratitude for sharing this simple, life-changing process. And you are just scratching the surface. Wait till you see what is to come.

Chapter Fifteen

Psychological Healing

"You must have failed deeply on some level or experienced some deep loss or pain to be drawn to the spiritual dimension. Or perhaps your very success became empty and meaningless and so turned out to be a failure."
- Ekhart Tolle -

"The disappointment you experience when things don't turn out as you wanted them to, become aware of that! That is freedom."
- Anthony de Mello -

Up till now we have been focusing on applying Quantum Entrainment to physical conditions. As remarkable as that is, there's more. Emotional QE is a powerful tool for quieting psychological pain. Like physical disharmony, psychological discordance can be removed instantly. Psychological pain may have it roots deeply embedded in what our mind perceives as our past. Quantum Entrainment does not recognize the past, or even the future. Both concepts are illusions and bind the mind to the ever-deepening spiral of entropy. That is to say, the flow of time is created in the mind. This fixation on what was and what will be plants the seed for psychological disease. That seed can only germinate and flourish under the watchful eye of father time.

According to quantum physics, time does not flow. The

arrow of time points in the direction of decay. The arrow points but does not move, much like a compass needle points north but does not move in that direction. It is the sweep of our consciousness that creates the illusion of time. Here's what I mean.

Emotional QE is a powerful tool for quieting psychological pain.

I love to go to the movies. For a couple of hours I become completely engrossed in the obvious illusion unfolding on the screen. When I step into that theatre I leave my everyday life behind. Although the movie is only a flickering of light and shadow, it represents the greater illusion we call "real life" waiting for us just outside the theatre doors.

The illusion of movement is created in our minds when thought oscillates between past and future. Thoughts of future and past construct a mental bridge crossing over the ever-present now of pure awareness. Our consciousness flits from thought to thought missing the pure awareness in between. It is like watching a movie. Movie film is a long strip of individual pictures or frames. In a single second 24 still frames flash on the screen. This is faster than our brains can individually process and so it looks like the still pictures are in motion. That is pretty amazing. We see motion where there is none. That is the illusion that a movie produces.

Our consciousness flits from thought to thought missing the pure awareness in between.

Likewise, time is the illusion that the mind produces.

Individual thoughts are like the individual frames of movie film. You will remember, individual thoughts break away from pure awareness and travel to our screen of consciousness. They occur so quickly they appear to be moving just like the individual frames of a movie. That illusion of motion is what we call time.

When we think about future events we are moving forward in time. When we visit our memories we are moving back in time. All this movement takes place in the mind. It exists nowhere else in this universe but in your mind. Even though it appears otherwise, your time, your future and your past, is not shared by anyone else.

The movie projector works on a simple principle. A bright white light shines through the film and creates a picture on the screen in the front of the theatre. The movement of the film, frame by frame through the light, creates the illusion of movement on the screen. As the audience, we sit contentedly watching the drama of the actors unfold, forgetting that they are merely light and shadow created by a bright light shining through film at the back of the theatre. We cry and we laugh as if the illusion were real.

Our life is just like a movie. It unfolds thought-by-thought, minute-by-minute, year-by-year. We, the audience, get completely absorbed in the drama of our own movie. We worry over the bills, love the new house, watch the children grow up, contemplate our own death. Like a movie, our lives are an illusion, a play of light and shadow. Don't get me wrong. Our lives exist, but not the way we think they do. This mistaken identity causes an overwhelming suffering that only deepens with each generation.

Our life is just like a movie. It unfolds thought-by-thought,
minute-by-minute, year-by-year.

Emotional Quantum Entrainment stops the mind in its tracks. It makes the mind pay attention to right now, robbing it of its preoccupation with past and future, robbing it of its guilt and anger, anxiety and fear. When we triangulate psychological discord we shine the bright light of pure awareness on it. This instantly takes us out of our movie mode. It takes us momentarily off the screen and places us in the audience. There we can observe the disharmonious emotions and events with healing calm and clarity. The movie of our life continues to unfold as before but without the influence of those hurtful, afflictive emotions.

The movie of our life continues to unfold as before but without
the influence of those hurtful, afflictive emotions.

How Emotional QE Works

Removing psychological pain is as easy as removing physical pain, perhaps easier. We don't even have to know what is causing the emotional distress in our partner. In fact, I strongly recommend that you allow your partner to keep her emotional concerns private. This practice is important in two ways. First, it affords your partner a level of privacy that may be welcome especially if she does not know you well or if she just wants to keep her inner life private. Second, you are saved from having to deal with someone else's emotions. This can be draining on your own emotions. And at the very least you will save time.

Emotional QE is completely safe. It is not a therapy of any

kind. It does not require analysis or training because the initiator does not do anything. Healing is accomplished by the partner bathing her emotional discord in the healing waters of pure awareness. The initiator just gets the process started, that's it. You do not have to muck around in a roiling sea of raw emotions. Leave that to the professionals.

Removing psychological pain is as easy as removing physical pain, perhaps easier.

Speaking of professionals, if you are a trained psychiatrist, psychologist or psychotherapist, you can use Emotional QE with great effectiveness in your practice. You may consider doing Emotional QE right after your initial pre-testing. Many initial sources of distress may be eliminated with little effort and you can then focus on what is left with more traditional techniques. Emotional QE will also work wonders for established patients. It can sometimes help break through long-standing blocks and will accelerate the healing process in general.

I once had a partner who was a psychologist with 25 years experience. I was able to initiate a life-altering change in her in just a few minutes. She had been lugging this trauma around with her since childhood. She had approached its solution from many different directions with quite a number of therapists throughout her professional career. Those few minutes of Emotional QE ended over six years ago and she is still emotionally free from this problem. It will not return.

The healing that takes place through Emotional QE is permanent. Fear is the basal emotion from which all others are spawned. Fear, as you remember, is created when ego appears to split from pure awareness and takes on its individual identity. It does not matter if your partner is experiencing anger, anxiety, guilt or sadness, at the bottom of it all is the fear of separation from pure awareness. Emotional QE floods fear with fullness, returning ego to mother's arms. The memory remains a ripple of awareness but the debilitating emotion is merged into an ocean of bliss.

The healing that takes place through Emotional QE is permanent.

How to Apply Emotional QE

First let your partner know that you do not have to know about his psychological pain. Let him know that it is pure awareness that does the healing. You only get the process started. He can keep his emotional discord private.

Ask him to think about the incident that is creating the distress. If there is no clear incident then have him privately identify the emotion. Then encourage him to allow his emotions to grow stronger. When they can get no stronger, ask your partner to grade the emotional discomfort 1 – 10, the 10 being unbearable. Remember his pre-test number.

Proceed as you did when removing physical problems with QE. (*See Triangulation: The Three-Step QE Process* above.) First, find a tight or tender muscle for Contact A. Then find Contact B. Become acutely aware of contact A, then B, then both together. Wait for your Eufeeling to surface and hold awareness of all three until you feel your partner's muscles relaxing under your touch.

When you have finished the session give your partner some time to reorient. Emotional QE may sometimes require a little more time than QE applied to physical complaints. As soon as your partner is ready, have him bring up the same incident and grade it 1 – 10. Partners usually express that they cannot even bring the emotion to mind. Or they will say, "I'm trying but all I can get is a 1 or a 2." You can see their facial muscles have relaxed and there is serenity in their voice.

Emotional QE instantly removes uncomfortable emotions even when we don't know why they are there. Pure awareness is able to get to the root without conscious awareness. On occasion your partners may remember the offending event and mention it during the session. This is especially so when they discover a deeply buried childhood trauma. Don't put much emphasis on this. Ask them to remain silent and close their eyes if they like. The abhorrent emotion has already been neutralized by the time your partner has this memory. There is no value in spending any more time on it. You can feel content that you were able to inspire a healing of your partner's emotional conflict and our troubled world is one candle brighter.

Emotional QE instantly removes uncomfortable emotions
even when we don't know why they are there.

Chapter Sixteen

Remote QE

"He who knows best knows how little he knows.
He who knows nothing is closer to the truth…"
- Thomas Jefferson -

"All truths are easy to understand once they are discovered;
the point is to discover them."
- Galileo Galilei -

Remote QE is performing Quantum Entrainment on partners without touching them. You can do Remote QE across the room or across the world. I recently had occasion to work with a partner in Salzburg, Austria. As the crow flies, a considerable distance from my office in Sarasota, Florida.

Maria, a student in Salzburg, was experiencing anxiety and always felt rushed. She told me, "From the time I wake up till the time I fall asleep I feel like I am studying for a final exam." We communicated through email. I never talked to her nor did I know what she looked like. All I had were e-words in an email.

You can do Remote QE across the room or across the world.

Maria wanted relief from her constant anxiety. She wanted a more directed energy to replace the hectic, erratic animation that defined her life. I performed Remote QE in the evening in Sarasota which turned out to be around 4 am in Salzburg. When I booted up my trusty ol' laptop the next morning, I was greeted by Maria's response. I include it here with only minor grammatical edits although maybe I should have taken out a few of the exclamation points.

Dear Frank,

I want to thank you so much for your help!!! I want to tell you, that when I got up this morning, it was the first time since a long period I had the feeling "to own all the energy of the world." I mean I felt so much energy and power and also when I was jogging this morning I had a lot of positive thoughts and energy. So something changed and I enjoyed and still enjoy it!!!!

THANK YOU!!!!

Hopefully you understand my English, it's not perfect ;-)

Vielen Dank and a lot of sunshine and greetings from Salzburg

Maria

The entity that is Maria is made of the same stuff as the

entity Frank. Pure awareness is not confined by time or space. It is everywhere, all the time. It is only our limited conception, our "me," that creates time and limits space. I inspired a healing event in the entity Maria by perceiving how we are the same, not how we are different. The sameness is pure awareness. When you practice QE you work from the level of ultimate sameness to effect healing changes in the world of differences.

I inspired a healing event in the entity Maria by perceiving how we are the same, not how we are different.

In quantum physics this instantaneous interaction at a distance is called entanglement. However, entanglement cannot transmit information faster than light. Whether the healing information that was transmitted to Maria was faster than the speed of light I cannot say. It is a fascinating discussion but way outside the scope of this short manuscript. For our purposes here it really doesn't matter. Somehow healing information found its way 5,000 miles to Maria's doorstep and didn't have to stop for direction on the way. That is good enough for me.

One more thing I'd like to mention before we learn how to do Remote QE. If you find Remote QE impossible to believe, don't worry about it. You will still be able to do it no matter what you believe. Quantum Entrainment is a scientifically reproducible procedure. It is real. It does not need belief to work. And if you don't believe that, ask any pain-free pets if they were asked to believe Quantum Entrainment before they were healed.

Quantum Entrainment is a scientifically reproducible procedure. It does not need belief to work.

Frank J Kinslow

How to do Remote QE

Basically you will triangulate as you have in the other forms of Quantum Entrainment. The basics are the same with some minor adaptations. Obviously we have to compensate for the lack of a physical partner. Remote QE is infinitely easier to learn than other activities where you need a partner. For some obscure reason the tango comes to mind. Oh well. Here are a few suggestions.

Use a Surrogate

A surrogate is a replacement, someone who takes the place of our partner. Any warm body will do -- your spouse or kids, the paperboy, the guy in the next cubicle. Just perform Remote QE on the physically present surrogate as if your absent partner were standing right in front of you. Make sure your intention includes the name, image or idea of your missing partner.

You can also use a pet as a surrogate. They usually make good stand-ins because they don't ask questions. They are used to the strange behavior of their masters and will probably submit willingly as long as there is a snack waiting for them at the end of the session. Although admittedly it may take quick fingers and box of Band-Aids if your only pet is a ravenous piranha. The upside is the snack would be provided during the QE session rather than afterward.

A third kind of surrogate can be a doll or stuffed animal. Actually, you can even draw a picture on a piece of paper and use that. Or just write your partner's name. All of these replacements will work just fine. Give it a try. You'll be pleasantly surprised.

Imagination

If you have a pretty active imagination you can conjure up a mental image of your partner and triangulate the image. Your fingers will not touch actual flesh so you will have to imagine that too. How do you know when to stop? You will feel the relaxation or melting under your imaginary fingers just as you do your physical ones.

Imagination QE can be done in a couple of ways. You can imagine you are where your partner is. Imagine her sitting in her favorite chair while you apply Remote QE. Another option is to bring your partner to you. Imagine her right there in front of you while you work your magic. Or you can meet any place you like. Literally, you are limited only by your imagination.

Air QE

You've heard of air guitar, pretending to hold the neck of a guitar while you pick and strum and gyrate wildly in front of the mirror? Well air QE is a little like that. Standing or sitting, imagine your partner in front of you. Whether your eyes are open or closed is completely up to you. Now physically move your body and reach out your hands to place your fingers on your absent partner. You do everything just as if your partner were there. Just don't let your spouse walk by in the middle of the session. Lucy you got some splaaaanen to do.

Remote QE is a wonderful way to get in all the QE practice you need. I do a session nightly before I go to bed. I usually have a list of people who have asked for help during the day. I also include partners who need continued care with chronic or life-threatening illnesses like Alzheimer's and cancer. Friends who thought regular Quantum Entrainment was weird now regularly call and ask for Remote QE.

My youngest daughter is a police officer in a very economically depressed and crime-ridden city. She is always getting into a scuffle of one sort or another. I'm no longer surprised when I get a call and she says, "Hey Dad, I was putting a woman on PCP in the cruiser when she bit a chunk of flesh out of my leg. Could you QE me tonight?" or "I tore my shoulder up again in a foot pursuit. How about working on the pain and range of motion for me?" Ah the joys of being a parent.

With practice, you will soon be able to Remote QE anytime there is a break in your day. I've even done it while the partner is describing his problem. By the time he finishes his pain has disappeared. It is absolutely wonderful to be so close to the creative force and watch it work its wonders. Our only limits are our unaware minds. And Quantum Entrainment will fix that.

How to Perform QE on Yourself

You already know how to work the wonders of Quantum Entrainment on yourself. Just pick a method already described and apply it to you. Of course, it helps to have the home edition of *Twister: for Double-Jointed Yoga Masters* if you want to work physically on your back or other hard-to-reach places. But remember, you don't have to contact the affected area. If you have mid-back pain you can physically set up on your knee or chest and be equally effective. Also consider using one of the Remote QE techniques mentioned above.

Wade, a QE practitioner, has found Quantum Entrainment

very helpful in his practice of yoga. He explains how he does it:

Since learning about Quantum Entrainment, I have used it on myself while practicing yoga. I find that I am going deeper into the asanas (poses), and going more quickly into stillness or still point consciousness while practicing yoga. In place of using my hands to triangulate on my body, I used awareness to connect the three points. Then I just relax into pure awareness for a few seconds. Following this, my body seems re-organized, refreshed, relaxed and stronger. This application of Quantum Entrainment can be used in any situation, and can facilitate a shift in identification from limited body-mind consciousness to infinite pure awareness.

The potential for QE is limited only by your imagination. It is our nature to expand and grow. Put on your QE glasses and have a look around. Experiment, play with different ideas but most of all have fun.

The potential for QE is limited only by your imagination.

Animals and Inanimate Objects

Because Quantum Entrainment draws from the most basic and all permeating pure awareness, it should work on animals and even inanimate objects. And it does! It's not all that strange when you think about it. We give medicines or chiropractic adjustments to our pets. But when it comes to so-called inanimate objects, I guess it is a bit of a stretch to think that we could pour a can of Red Bull into our depleted car battery to give it new life. I say "so-called" inanimate objects because all of creation is vibrating with life on the subtlest level. Nothing is inanimate in the ultimate sense. And within the subtlest vibration exists its cause, pure awareness. So when it comes to a dead car battery QE is cheaper than Red Bull and there is no can to recycle.

Nothing is inanimate in the ultimate sense.

One of our workshop graduates reported that he had a dead car battery. He made a number of unsuccessful attempts to start his car by turning the key in the ignition. Then he QE'ed the battery. The car kicked right over and the engine purred to life. When he took the car into the shop his mechanic said that the battery was indeed the culprit. He probably didn't mention to the mechanic that the jumper cables he used were his fingers.

Quantum Entrainment has universal influence and that includes household appliances. I love this blender story from a creative QE'er.

I wanted to share my experience with Quantum Entrainment after attending the workshop. I woke up Sunday really hungry. So I applied the QE to my hunger, and the hunger left. I still decided I wanted to make a smoothie. Just when I was about to start blending the smoothie, the blender motor didn't work. It was completely dead. So I decided to apply the QE to the blender. I worked with it for a few seconds...nothing. I tried the QE again, this time completely letting go of a desired outcome. It worked!!! The blender was back to normal, and I got to enjoy my smoothie while being completely humbled by the experience. My roommate, who also loves smoothies, is amazed when I zap the blender before each use.

Since your partner does not have to believe in QE to get the results, animals respond beautifully to Quantum Entrainment. Apply QE to your pet problems or even pesky varmints like over-enthusiastic raccoons, dogs and bothersome bears. At a recent book signing at the I Am Healing Arts Center by best-selling author of Chicken Soup for the Woman's Soul, Jennifer Hawthorne, the air conditioners were not working and the doors had to be opened. Uninterested in having their book signed, a dozen or so large black flies made a beeline for the huge pot of chicken soup on the snack table. Rob, manager of the center, made a beeline for a nearby meditation room and QE'ed the little buggers. When he emerged from the room a few minutes later there was but a single fly buzzing around. When he saw Rob materialize from the adjoining room, the fly exited quickly stage left.

Animals respond beautifully to Quantum Entrainment.

Food offers another area of exploration for creative QE'ers. You might consider entraining your groceries, water and nutritional supplements. Your intention might be to potentiate the beneficial ingredients, remove toxins or improve digestion and assimilation before a meal is eaten. If you say grace before a meal, then add Quantum Entrainment at the end of your prayer. In this way, the prayer becomes your intention and QE takes that intention and lays it at the omnipresent feet of pure awareness.

Chapter Seventeen

Extended QE

"Those who wish to sing always find a song."
- Plato -

"Joy is not in things, it is in us."
- Richard Wagner -

Extended QE is valuable for chronic, long-standing or life-threatening health concerns like diabetes, heart disease, Alzheimer's or cancer. It is also especially effective at soothing and healing deep emotional conflicts. When a malady does not respond after several minutes or several attempts with Quantum Entrainment then it is a candidate for Extended QE.

As the name would imply, we are extending the usual time of QE, thus profoundly increasing the benefits to partner and initiator alike. When Extended QE is performed awareness is held in the depths of pure awareness and the common world of cars, stars, people and even space becomes supersaturated with pure awareness. Pure awareness becomes almost tangible, a healing salve of vibrant renewal.

> *Extended QE is valuable for chronic, long-standing*
> *or life-threatening health concerns...*

Some years ago, when I was first developing Quantum Entrainment, I was asked to lunch by an acquaintance and fellow chiropractor. He said he had a favor to ask so when I arrived at the restaurant I approached his table with some anticipation. When I looked into Mark's normally energetic brown eyes I saw a deep, sinking sadness. We greeted each other and while we waited for the waitress we exchanged pleasantries and caught up on the doings of our colleagues. We ordered, and while we waited for our lunch to arrive he became pensive. He started to speak, halted then looked down at his salad. I waited. He raised his head and tears had pooled in his eyes. I looked at him, encouraging him to continue with my eyes. He began again, "My wife has been fighting cancer for more than a year. She has fought hard but yesterday she was admitted to the hospital. She has two malignant tumors. The one in her uterus is the size of a walnut. The one in her liver is the size of a grapefruit. She is not expected to come home again.

"I know you do some kind of faith healing or meditation or something like that," he said, "and I wonder if you could help Jillie." I had never met his wife but I agreed to go to the hospital that evening and meet with her. I asked him to talk to the nursing staff to see if I could have an uninterrupted hour alone with her. I also asked that no family be present during the last hour of visiting hours when I planned to arrive. He agreed. We finished our meal in relative silence and I returned to my afternoon patients.

That evening I met Mark outside his wife's room. He told me that the nursing staff had been somewhat resistant to the idea of me doing anything "weird" but they agreed to give us the time we needed. I paused outside her room then pushed open the heavy door and walked into a dark and cheerless place.

The first thing I remember was the smell. It was not the smell of death but of the dying. I can't describe it but it penetrates the mind and dampens the spirit. Jillie was asleep. She was a slight woman with weak, blonde hair tangled across her pillow. I didn't wake her but started Extended QE immediately.

Not five minutes later a nurse came in to take Jillie's vitals and move a few things around then left. Ten minutes later she was back and 10 minutes after that someone else interrupted us for no apparent reason other than make sure everything was in order. I thought I had inadvertently discovered a magical spell that could make nurses appear out of thin air in a busy hospital. I finished the hour with Jillie, who would wake occasionally only to fall back into a fitful sleep. Although Mark had told her I was coming, I don't think she recognized me or my mission.

I returned the next night to pretty much the same routine from the staff but Jillie was more alert and we had several brief exchanges throughout the hour. Despite the interruptions I was able to hold pure awareness for most of the hour. I left feeling lighter and somehow inspired.

When I arrived on the third night there was a handwritten note on Jillie's door that said "Do Not Enter" and it was signed by the head nurse on the evening shift. My first thought was that I was being ousted by a hostile staff fueled by ignorance about non-allopathic "alternative" healing. I felt that this prejudice would be harmful to their patient and should not be tolerated. I marched over to the nurse's station and asked rather heatedly, "Why am I being kept from seeing Jillie?"

The answer shocked me. The nurse smiled kindly and said that the sign was for my and Jillie's benefit. It was put on the door so that we would not be disturbed. She told me that the nurses on all shifts had seen a remarkable change in Jillie's condition. They didn't know if what I was doing was the reason, but they could assure me that my time in the room would be uninterrupted. And they were true to their word. It turns out that the prejudice was all mine.

I continued to perform Extended QE with Jillie every evening after seeing patients. Her room lost the feel and smell of death. Jillie was more alert and, although we spoke infrequently in short, soft phrases, we started developing a nonverbal bond of inner knowing. The regular and sustained practice of quantum wakefulness had benefits for me as well. I found more peace and compassion growing in my life. I felt that I was blossoming somehow, awakening to a kind of immortality free of the fear of death.

The morning after my eighth visit I took a call from Mark. He told me that I didn't have to visit Jillie in the hospital that evening because she was being released. He told me that the tumor in her uterus was gone and the grapefruit- size tumor in her liver was now the size of a walnut. I asked if he would like me to go to their home and continue with Extended QE. He told me that Jillie said I should take some time off. She said that she could handle it from there.

Freed from her hospital bed, Jillie completely devoted her life to her family. I was invited to be a part of the family and made a couple of the gatherings but we gradually lost track of each other. Over time the cancer slowly returned. I offered to resume our Quantum Entrainment sessions but Jillie refused. Her words surprised me but her voice told me that she was at peace. She quietly passed away at home, surrounded by her family. Mark later told me that Jillie believed that her "second life" was a godsend and the happiest of her times in this world.

Extended QE is remarkably powerful. And it is especially important to remember that pure awareness knows what needs to be done. Because it is human nature, we feel the need for stronger desire and more effort when working with life-threatening conditions. It is easy to forget that we are initiators with a simple intention and that is all. Healing will take place or it won't. That is out of our hands. The severity of the condition does not call for stronger intentions or more effort. Simple innocence is called for, nothing more.

Extended QE is remarkably powerful.

How to Extend QE

An Extended QE session can last from five minutes to an hour or so. Twenty minutes seems about right for most of my sessions. Although I will lengthen or shorten the time as needed.

Start an Extended QE session exactly as you would the regular Quantum Entrainment session of one or two minutes. I like to start out standing and then have my partner sit a couple of minutes later. Extended QE can also be done lying down, especially if your partner is quite ill.

There are some minor differences with Extended QE that should be noted. To start, hold your contact points and wait for your Eufeeling. Once you get the initial relaxation or dissolving sensation that signals the end of regular QE, continue to hold your Eufeeling. You can forget about being aware of your contact fingers and simply be aware of your Eufeeling. From time to time your mind will wander. When you realize that it is elsewhere, again become aware of your Eufeeling. Your original Eufeeling will more than likely change. You may first experience stillness or peace which may give way to bliss or joy or even ecstasy. Whatever Eufeeling is there' just be aware of it.

Every few minutes, when the notion strikes you, move your contact fingers to other parts of your partner's body. Common places for Extended QE are the forehead, temples, heart, and solar plexus although any appropriate area of the body will do just fine. As soon as your fingers find their new position return to your Eufeeling and settle in for the next few minutes.

During the lengthened session you can occasionally restate or rephrase your intention. This keeps the mind lively and on point. You may also naturally see with your "inner vision" your intention at work. You may see joints healing or lungs opening to receive life-giving air. You may see or feel other healing forces at work. Don't get involved. Whatever you witness just let it unfold on its own. You have a front row seat as the healing impulses of pure awareness rise up and take form. You are the innocent witness to creation and re-creation. Nothing you do can improve on that. Know that this time is special and you are blessed to be the silent witness.

You may also see geometric symbols or the flowing and swirling of abstract energies at work within you and your partner's body. The heavens may open and golden light may shower down on you. Angels may sing and blow their trumpets to herald the coming healing. Your job? Just take it all in. Don't get caught up in the symbolism or symptomatology of it all. Just be there and enjoy the ever-growing, healing presence of pure awareness.

Know that this time is special and
you are blessed to be the silent witness.

When the Extended QE session is over allow at least two or three minutes for your partners to open their eyes and return to activity. That is a minimum. They may fully need 5 or 10 minutes or even require lying down afterward. Make sure to let them know that if they get tired later in the day that they should rest and certainly should get a good night's sleep.

As with the shorter QE, the healing that is started during Extended QE will continue for a day or two afterward. On occasion, your partner may feel tired or "emotional" the following day. This is an indication that very deep healing is taking place and, if at all possible, your partner should rest, eat well and take light exercise.

I rely heavily on Extended QE in my counseling practice. It is a remarkably potent purifier of emotions and healer of the body. And, of course, I love it for what it does for me. I will continue to rely on it until I experience that final paradigm shift that allows me to walk through walls or float featherlike through the air. Until that happens, and I'll certainly let you know when it does, it's Quantum Entrainment in all its variations for me.

Chapter Eighteen

User-Friendly World Peace

"Every society by its own practice of living and by the mode of relatedness, of feelings, and perceiving, develops a system of categories which determines the forms of awareness."
- Erich Fromm -

"Now there is one outstandingly important fact regarding Spaceship Earth, and that is that no instruction book came with it."
- Buckminster Fuller -

I just want to take a few minutes to thank you for dropping by and spending this time with me. I am continually inspired by you, and the thousands of people like you who have opened your minds to the possibility of the impossible. I want Quantum Entrainment to work for you. I have QE'ed this book with that intention. I want you to be completely successful, and that is not entirely altruistic on my part. Every time you do QE I benefit; the whole world benefits. If you don't see that now you soon will. My challenge, my plea to you is a simple one: practice QE and spread the healing power of pure awareness quickly and fully amongst your fellow human beings. You, being closest to the fire of awareness, will harvest the most benefit. But all of us will reap the rewards of your simple effort. And as more of us perform Quantum Entrainment each of us will become more success-ful and more fulfilled in every avenue of our lives. As we think, so we live. Thinking "outside the box," a term I hope will soon fall into disuse, should be the norm. In fact, thinking based on boundlessness has to become commonplace to insure the safety and sanity of our race. That humankind is struggling to survive is no news flash. We have been inching our way toward oblivion for generations. Each discordant thought we create is like one more grain of sand added to the quicksand that is slowly dragging us down. This, of course, is insanity. You know insanity; doing the same thing and expecting different results. Our new world will not come from documents and proclamations. It cannot unfold out of the common and collective consciousness that has dominated human thought to this point. It will not come from outside, but from deep within where perfect awareness awaits.

Each discordant thought we create is like one more grain of sand added to the quicksand that is slowly dragging us down.

Now I know it seems just a little grandiose to suggest that a simple healing process can save our collective bacon but it can, for it is not the process proper but the awareness we bring to the task which wields the ultimate power. You have seen that for yourself. Awareness heals. The more aware we are the more healing unfolds in and around us. It does so naturally, spontaneously and without effort.

We, collectively known as the human race, have but a single lesson to learn: be aware. We are continually being reminded to "live in the present." But what does that mean? Does it mean that we stop planning for the future or give up our memories? Of course not. Living in the "now" is living in pure awareness. Pure awareness extinguishes psychological time, freeing the mind from the need to do, allowing it to reflect timeless and perfect order. An aware mind is organized, energetic and creative. An aware mind is peaceful. It can do no harm.

We, collectively known as the human race, have
but a single lesson to learn: be aware.

Carl Jung's collective unconscious and more recently Rupert Sheldrake's morphic field illustrate a vital point about being human. As it turns out we are not isolated entities aimlessly rambling around in a body/mind. We have an infinitely intimate relationship with every other soul on this planet. Every one of our thoughts and actions influences every other breathing being.

Thoughts are charged clouds that attract other thoughts of like charge. The more people think similar thoughts the more momentum these clouds of consciousness gather. This is what Sheldrake calls a morphic field. Not only do we feed into these morphic fields but we are also influenced by them. You can see that what we think and experience is very important. If you have ever wondered why people keep performing the same damaging behavior you have your answer in the morphic field.

The most powerful, life-supporting morphic field is one created by individuals who are experiencing pure awareness. This brings us to my point about user friendly world peace. Quantum Entrainment has enormous value as a healing procedure, but that is just the tip of the iceberg. When even a small percentage of people become clearly aware, it positively influences the minds and lives of everyone, even those who are not reflecting pure awareness. That's right, even as little as one per cent of a population reflecting the coherency of pure awareness can have profound effects on their immediate surroundings, from there spreading to awaken the whole world. This is not some fanciful philosophy but scientific fact.

Beginning in the early 1960s, the Transcendental Meditation organization demonstrated the "one percent effect." They were able to confirm that if only one percent of a city's population were experiencing the coherency of pure awareness, the crime rate would drop. They would take a small number of TM mediators into a city and, as a group, simply become aware. Using the FBI's crime statistics for 22 cities, the group was able to reduce significantly the overall crime rate by an average of 24 percent! Since then there have been numerous other studies to show how focused awareness alone can change our lives for the better.

In her book *The Intention Experiment*, Lynne McTaggart presents a number of sound scientific studies that support this very point. McTaggart even gives us the number of aware people it would take to create a wave of coherency in the United States and the world. Are you ready for this? To immediately create a healthier, cleaner, more loving life for all the inhabitants of the United States, it will only take 1,730 aware people. To have peace and prosperity spread throughout the world we will only need 8,084 people practicing awareness. We literally have the technology to save our world right at our fingertips.

We literally have the technology to save our world right at our fingertips.

The Quantum Entrainment process has the power to heal your world locally. But that influence is not confined to just you and your immediate concerns. When you practice Quantum Entrainment your soothing influence instantly radiates outward to help heal the ills of us all. I forget the name of the French philosopher who said that just the simple act of bending over and picking a flower changes the center of gravity of the entire universe. It's no different when you create a QE healing event. Every time you perform QE, you plant a seed that will produce a blossom of the greatest rarity. Like dropping a pebble in a quiet pond, your healing touch will send peaceful ripples that will gently rock the distant shores of every universe. Every time you create a QE healing event you make the world a better place to live in.

Of course Quantum Entrainment is not the only way to awareness. There are thousands of roads to inner peace and outer harmony. I am making a plea for all of us to become more aware every day, as often as we can. QE is simple, instantaneous and fun. It has immediate practical benefits as well as long-standing effects on body, mind and environment. It doesn't require that you set aside a time and place to practice. You can do it anytime, anywhere. Additionally, Quantum Entrainment doesn't just ask you to sit in awareness. QE teaches you to move through that fullness, amplifying its profundity and quickly establishing it in your day-to-day life. These advantages make QE the perfect practice for the monk, the mogul or the single mother of three. Do Quantum Entrainment throughout the day, every day. Do it by itself or add it to other self-awareness systems to increase their effectiveness. Add QE at the end of your meditations or prayers, business meetings, while you are stuck in traffic or waiting in the "10 Items or Less" lane with arms full of last-minute dinner items. Do this simple thing and witness first-hand a miraculous transformation it will bring to your life.

If you don't believe what I am saying can possibly be true then you must take the challenge. For if I am wrong, we humans have painted ourselves into a dreadfully bleak corner and you have nothing to lose. Even so, you still have a pretty remarkable tool for healing sprains, indigestion, broken hearts and the like. But if I am right, you will become one of the first to break into the light of a life of prosperity and peace. There is only one thing holding you back, a belief that it can't be so. The only belief that you have to overcome is the one stopping you from taking the first step. After that it's easy. I'm reminded of a short discourse between Alice and the White Queen from Lewis Carroll's, Through the Looking Glass.

> "There is no use trying," said Alice, "one can't believe impossible things."
> "I dare say you haven't had much practice," said the Queen.
> "When I was your age, I always did it for half an hour a day. Why, sometimes I've believed as many as six impossible things before breakfast."

I am not even asking you to change your beliefs. Beliefs don't change our world, awareness does. So keep your beliefs intact if you like; but be aware. Awareness will allow you to keep those beliefs that work and will softly dissolve those that don't simultaneously serve you and this world.

Practice Quantum Entrainment often, with a playful sense of purpose. Become a child exploring your world, eyes wide open. When was the last time, in this feverish world, you gave in to the magic of the moment? Do you remember the joy of lying on your back in the grass watching altogether white clouds slide lazily across a deep blue sky? You may not have recognized then the pure awareness that spawned in you the deep sense of peace and joy. Now that you know pure awareness, let it enfold you completely in its arms. Help yourself to what is already yours. Heal your world, and therein heal our world, one soul at a time.

Contact Frank at: *www.QuantumEntrainment.org.*

While you are there, catch up on the latest QE news and events; make an appointment for a private Extended QE session with Frank or pick up a copy of his first book, *Beyond Happiness: How You Can Fulfill Your Deepest Desire.* By all means, stop by the QE blog and find out how others are using Quantum Entrainment to create harmony and healing in their lives. While there, ask your questions and share your QE thoughts and experiences. We'd love to hear from you. Then, don't be a stranger. Visit us often and become a part of this dynamic and exciting movement building world peace through individual peace.

Breinigsville, PA USA
04 April 2010
235505BV00001B/15/P

9 780615 226804